Accounting for Small Business

A Handbook to Launching a Successful Small Business, Learn Accounting and Bookkeeping Principles

By

Owen Solomon

© **Copyright 2020 by Owen Solomon - All rights reserved.**

This document is geared towards providing exact and reliable information in regards to the topic and issue covered. The publication is sold with the idea that the publisher is not required to render accounting, officially permitted, or otherwise, qualified services. If advice is necessary, legal or professional, a practiced individual in the profession should be ordered.

- From a Declaration of Principles which was accepted and approved equally by a Committee of the American Bar Association and a Committee of Publishers and Associations.

In no way is it legal to reproduce, duplicate, or transmit any part of this document in either electronic means or in printed format. Recording of this publication is strictly prohibited and any storage of this document is not allowed unless with written permission from the publisher. All rights reserved.

The information provided herein is stated to be truthful and consistent, in that any liability, in terms of inattention or otherwise, by any usage or abuse of any policies, processes, or directions contained within is the solitary and utter responsibility of the recipient reader. Under no circumstances will any legal responsibility or blame be held against the publisher for any reparation, damages, or monetary loss due to the information herein, either directly or indirectly.

Respective authors own all copyrights not held by the publisher.

The information herein is offered for informational purposes solely, and is universal as so. The presentation of the information is without contract or any type of guarantee assurance.

The trademarks that are used are without any consent, and the publication of the trademark is without permission or backing by the trademark owner. All trademarks and brands within this book are for clarifying purposes only and are the owned by the owners themselves, not affiliated with this document.

Table Of Contents

INTRODUCTION 6

CHAPTER 01: HOW TO BECOME AN ENTREPRENEUR? 11

1.1 Getting Started With a Small Business 12

1.2 Finding a Small Business 17

1.3 Financing Your Small Business 26

1.4 Determining Feasibility of a Small Business 29

1.5 How to Promote Your Small Business? 32

CHAPTER 02: RUNNING A SMALL SUCCESSFUL BUSINESS 36

2.1 Business Planning: Key to Success 38

2.2 Outsourcing 44

2.3 Simplifying Your Accounting 46

2.4 Managing Your Expenses 50

2.5 Developing a Marketing Plan 54

2.6 Keeping Customers Loyal 59

CHAPTER 03: KEEPING YOUR BOOKS 64

3.1 How to Keep Your Books? 64

3.2 Why Is It Important To Keep Books? 66

3.3 Difference Between Book-Keeping and Accounting 69

CHAPTER 04: MANAGING PROFITABILITY AND CASH ... 73

4.1 Success or Failure, It Depends On Cash-flow 74

4.2 Making Sense of Financial Statements 77

4.3 Managing Your Inventory 85

4.4 Setting up Payrolls 92

4.5 Managing your Account Receivables and Creditors 97

4.6 Understanding Key ratios and Percentages 104

CHAPTER 05: TIPS FOR MANAGING YOUR GROWING BUSINESS ... 108

CONCLUSION ... 116

REFERENCES ... 119

Introduction

To those of us who have dreamed of participating in a small business, this book is all about you. This concept of "being your own boss" is undoubtedly an alluring one. Nonetheless, not everyone can be a boss-not one decent or effective, at least. If you are actually an employee of someone (not a boss), it is perfectly natural to fantasize about owning a business of your own on those days when you are fed up with your current boss or work. The rags-to-rich stories you hear about entrepreneurs, who have turned their visions into millions or even billions of dollars, make your fantasy even more attractive. But in the midst of your dreams, realize that there are some not-so-appealing dimensions of small business ownership as well. Most often, it takes many years of hard work and tons of hard choices before the risks you take a turn into rewards.

And, most of all, the entrepreneurial career can be solitary on top. The excitement of being the ultimate decision-maker may, of course, be exactly what draws you to small business in the first place, but you should know that this appeal has its downsides, the most prominent of which is that it encourages trial and error, and that trial and error beget errors. Mistakes are the most expensive (and the most dangerous) form of learning for small business owners.

There are many factors that affect how you start and run your own business, but I hope you will find this book as a handy guide for running a successful small business as well as basic accounting requirements. To some, it can be overwhelming to start a business, and to others, it is a case of; they can't wait to get started. Either way, it's always good to remember that there's plenty of help and advice out there, and that advice can be invaluable not only, but it also doesn't have to cost the earth. Treat all aspects of therapy into your company as an invaluable investment. Anyone trying to run their own business is an Entrepreneur because Entrepreneurs are taking resources and getting things done. That is exactly what you do when you run your own business.

Small business is not science about rockets. What you need is support, and that is precisely why this book is written. Aside from skills, successful entrepreneurs either possess many requisite traits or adopt them:

1. **Confidence:** Small business owners must be able to coexist with risk, and possibly debt. Capitalism offers no guarantees to its participants; therefore, the small business and consequently its owner are generally at risk and sometimes in debt. And yet, by night, its creator still has to sleep.

2. **Intuition:** Call it gut feeling or intuition; the small business owner has to call things right more often than wrong.

3. **Optimism:** Small business owners rarely see good fortune, not misfortune; upsides, not downsides; and opportunities, not problems. The small business owner can always hire the advocate of a devil (which is what counsel and accountants are for), but the enthusiasm and optimism needed to drive the vision must come from the entrepreneur.

4. **Drive:** Successful small business owners are driven to create a product, customer service and build a successful business. Unlike chocolate cravings, this urge isn't going away.

5. **Passion:** The passion of one entrepreneur is infectious. Your employees, your vendors, and your customers-whoever you come in contact with-can feel and feed your passion.

Does this mean you will sit on the receiving end of a paycheck if you don't have those five traits? Okay, let's start by saying we understand that being a good employee today often needs some of these qualities, so owning a business isn't just your preference. However, if you don't have most of these features in healthy supply, you'll probably be better off as an employee rather than a small business owner.

Yays and Nays of Having a Small Business

However, in this section, we are sticking with the best reasons why people choose to own a business:

1. **Creation satisfaction:** Have you ever experienced the pride of constructing a chair, preparing a gourmet meal, or repairing a vacuum cleaner? Or how about offering required counseling services to help people overcome their vexing financial issues? The small business owner is exposed every day to the excitement of production, not to mention the satisfaction of solving a problem for a customer.

2. **Establishment of their own culture:** No longer standing around the water cooler complaining about "the way things are around here." After you have started your own business, the way things are around here is a direct function of how you intend them to be.

3. **Consider financial upside:** Charles Schwab, Oprah Winfrey, and Steve Jobs. It's no wonder that these once small business owners are among the wealthiest individuals in the country. (A recent SBA report certainly concluded that although small business ownership is risky, small business owners were considerably more likely to be rated as high income and high wealth.)

4. **Self-sufficiency:** It has proved to be a less than gratifying task for many people to work for another. Many people have discovered as a result of such unfulfilled encounters that if they want to provide for themselves and their families, they'd better build the opportunity themselves. It

is either that, or it is willing to spend a long wait in the line of unemployment on occasion.

5. **Flexibility:** Perhaps you prefer to work in the evenings because that's when your partner is working, or you want to spend more time with the children during the day. Or you might prefer to take frequent three-day weekend jaunts instead of just a few full-week vacations each year. After all, you're the boss, and your schedule can usually be tailored to meet your personal needs as well as those of your customers.

Why would any reasonable soul elect to continue receiving a paycheck in the light of the resounding potential benefits? Why wouldn't all want to own a business? Let's have the nays counted:

1. **Responsibility:** Not only does your family depend on your business success as a small business owner, so do your partners, your employees, and their families, your customers, and sometimes your vendors. As much as we love our small businesses, even the most enthusiastic of us wax nostalgic every now and then for the good old days when we punched our time card and walked out of the door really, really, done for the day. Beware that another downside to running your own business is that you may be susceptible to becoming a workaholic if you are the type of person who sometimes assumes more responsibility than you can manage and works for too many hours.

2. **Competition:** While some people thrive on competition, the same rivalry returns to haunt you by threatening your health. You will soon find out that a host of hungry rivals are chasing your customers and challenging your future, by cutting prices or by providing a more complete package of unique services. Of course, competition is what makes capitalism go' round, but to have a competition, you

should note that somebody will win and somebody will lose.

3. **Change:** There are products and services coming and there are products and services going. In the business of doing business, nothing is sacred, and the pace of change today is significantly faster than it was a generation ago, and it shows no signs of slowing. If you don't like change and the commotion it creates, then perhaps better for you is the consistency a bigger, more hierarchical organization offers.

4. **Opportunity:** interest rates, economy, fraud, accident, natural disasters, disease, and the list continues. Any such random events can send reeling to your business.

5. **Red tape:** taxation, reforms of infrastructure, regulations, tariffs, sanctions, contracts, OSHA, FDA, NAFTA, etc.

6. **Business failure:** And finally, as if this list of enemies of a small business is not long enough, the owner faces the specter of the ultimate downside: bankruptcy in the form of business failure. This is the stage where the owner is standing back and watching the creditors dive into like vultures to devour their remaining assets.

In the first chapter of this book, you will learn all the basics of how to become a successful entrepreneur. And in the second chapter, you will learn how to actually run that small business in the light of success for a long period. And in the third chapter, you will find the answer to how you can keep your book records, and is it so important for an entrepreneur like you. And in the fourth chapter, you will learn all the basic accounting that you must be aware of when starting your own small business. And in the last chapter, there will be tips that will help you to be a better entrepreneur. Let's dig into this book.

Chapter 01: How to Become an Entrepreneur?

Anyone looking to run their own business is an Entrepreneur because Entrepreneurs are taking resources and getting things done. That is exactly what you do when you run your own business. But remember, it isn't just about having an idea. It's about getting it enforced. Drive and ambition are key ingredients in entrepreneurship. If there isn't really a demand for your idea, there's no point flying a dead horse just because you want to prove other people wrong. Entrepreneurs are more innovative, leading to the creation of new products and services, which in turn leads to reduced unemployment and an increase in lifestyles.

What's a successful entrepreneur, then?

It is generally acknowledged that an entrepreneur's attributes or traits are fundamental:

- Ambition (the need for success),
- Creativity (always innovative),
- Tenacity (often stubborn),
- Risk Tolerance (being bold),
- Intuition (spontaneous) and
- Personality (life and soul).

But not every small enterprise is positioned to succeed. In fact, only about two-thirds of employed businesses survive for at least two years, and about half survive for five years. The stage is often set at the start, so make sure you follow all the steps necessary when starting your business can lay the foundation for success.

1.1 Getting Started With a Small Business

All have dreamed of owning a business. We all have ideas that come into our minds at one time or another but never make it into the market place. It has been said that the following thinking can better describe an entrepreneur: Both people have great ideas while they're in the shower. Most of us get out and forget about the shower. The businessman is the person who gets off the shower and acts on those ideas. Yet if you ask yourself questions before you act, you can increase your chances of success. What is the reason for starting a small business? What type of business can I start? What skills, preferences, and personal qualities can I bring to the business? As a business owner, what are the strengths and weaknesses?

Examining Your Personal Objectives

Start with a look at why you want to start a small business. People come for a variety of reasons to become business owners. They want to be their own boss, build a future, and earn a lot of money too. See for yourself why you want to start and run a business. What are the factors which motivate you?

1. Choose a small business with a huge potential for profit. Why would you go into business, after all, if not to make a lot of money?

2. Choose a market you're in for. If you do not want to enjoy the work, why do you?

If your motivation is profit, take a closer look at what that means. A business must be able to cover all of its costs, pay all of its expenses, meet the personal financial needs of the owners, and have ample net income left to enable the business to grow. Will this small business deliver full income for you? Will Small Business add to your current income? Firstly, you need to look at your personal financial needs.

If your motivation is to do what you love, then try to analyze what that means. Is there a market to support your dreams in there? Is there enough revenue to make this business profitable, and not just folly? Is that feasible for your small business? You can develop a business with careful research and planning that fills a need, brings you pleasure and pride, and earns enough revenue to meet your personal needs, pay for itself, and provide profits for future growth. The keywords are Planning and Analysis.

Exploring Business Ideas

New small business ideas come in many ways. You can wish yours no turn and interest in a company. Take a look at your interests, volunteering, and leisure sports. You might be able to develop a line of specialty foods, plan events, give golf lessons, or develop an antique refinishing service.

Sell everything you say. Any specialized knowledge or skill can become a business. In your area of expertise, you can develop a newspaper column, write a book, present workshops, and hold seminars. An Internet understanding may lead to the design, monitoring, and updating of Web sites.

Business can be developed based on the equipment you already have and the technology you understand. Examples are video recording and special event photography. Many new businesses are started by people who make use of existing skills from their salaried work. When businesses scale down and outsource, new opportunities for entrepreneurs are growing.

You may wish to explore a new idea for yourself. Take classes, apprenticeships, or work in an area that addresses your new field of interest. If you think you may be interested in catering or some other food industry facet, work in a restaurant. Know all facets of the business. How are deliveries ordered, how are deliveries handled, how are inventory controlled, how are food handlers handled, and how are invoices and orders handled? What are the restaurant strengths? What'd you make better? You will not steal their business plan! You get an education while moonlighting, and you earn extra money to get your business started. You'll also find out whether you really like working with food.

Identifying Skills, Interest, and Personal Qualities

Now is the time to step back and take an objective look at what is in front of you. Business ownership is not for everybody. Although some people may have the motivation and desire for ownership of the business, they may not have taken the time to properly investigate and research their capabilities and business ideas. A careful assessment of your skills, interests, and personal qualities can help you determine the business that suits you best. Skills are your ability to make proficient use of your knowledge and your training. Value is what you like doing, and that gives you pleasure. Personal Qualities are the traits and features that make you unique.

a. Personality Type

Your personality should be compatible with your choice of small business. If you don't invest the time now to figure out what makes you happy and keeps you motivated every day, in the future, you might be very unhappy. But why does personality matter so? Learning about your personality allows you to reflect on your day-to-day emotions, behaviors, and ways of thinking. Do you prefer working alone, for example, or do you prefer to work with others? Would you be happy in a small company that requires you to be extremely organized and have a set schedule? Or are you the kind of person who likes a free, flexible schedule to encourage you to be spontaneous? This information will help you decide which small business matches your personality preferences.

b. Skills

In addition to personality, the skills in the small business process are also important to consider. If you've lived in the United States and served in colonial times, what expertise would you need to gain? What type of person would you want your employer to be? And how different would then be your competences, so aptitudes compared to today? Many industries that evolved during the 1600s-1700s, such as health care, publishing, manufacturing, construction, finance, and agriculture, are still with us today. And many of the same employers seek today are the professional skills, aptitudes, and values required in those industries.

Evaluating Your Strengths and Weakness

Identifying your strengths and weaknesses is not just an exercise to make you feel good (or bad) about yourself if you are thinking about starting a business, It's a framework that will allow you to understand how you can be most successful at what you are doing, and where you will need to change if you want to succeed.

1. First, create two lists

Before using any external sources to help identify your strengths and weaknesses, it is recommended that you spend some 30 minutes creating two lists alone. Your first list will focus on your corporate or entrepreneurial goals. Call it something like, "Skills Need to Success." Don't worry if you've considered any skills needed to succeed in your business. It may list things like "market awareness," "business development," "website development," or "product knowledge," depending on your business. Once you've completed the list, highlight the skills you already have, and put a star next to those you think you need to improve. Then, set aside this list, you'll return to it later.

Don't beat yourself over what you consider are big shortcomings, and don't overestimate how powerful your strengths are. Just write down them, and move on.

You don't need to have a full list of 100 strengths and weaknesses, either. If you have included more than 10-15 things in each list, then you are likely to start concentrating too much on strengths and weaknesses that aren't so important.

2. Talk to Persons You Trust

Many people think too highly or too little about themselves. Try to think of three to five people whose opinions you value, and who have had the opportunity to live or work with you for a long time to come. You want people that have witnessed your actions and character in various situations. It will include a significant other community for most individuals, perhaps a counselor or therapist, a best friend, one or more parents.

The length of your relationships is not the only thing to take into account. Whether or not you value or trust their opinion about you is the most important thing. Some friends and family members are going to be too biased — they either think that everything you do is stunning or in the past, their opinions have been hurtful and destructive. Choose people carefully with a good track record to be positive and supportive, even when they had to tell you something you didn't want to hear.

Once you have a select group of people, send them out. With each of them you can go out for a coffee, or just send an email with some questions and ask for their honest feedback.

Start adding more details to both of your lists as you receive feedback. Some of the strengths and weaknesses you've listed are validated by those you know, while others you've listed are not as important to the people who've been with you. Fine-tune the lists.

3. **Try New Things**

When you have a lack of experience, one difficulty with defining strengths and weaknesses comes up. You could look at your list of weaknesses in some situations and find that it mostly amounts to "I don't know, I've never tried." For example, how do you know if you have an athletic or artistic skill if you've never tried to do something athletic or artistic about it? Try new things, then. If you don't want to try out new things, then don't be a businessman.

1.2 Finding a Small Business

Many people believe in the mysterious process of starting a business. They know they want a business to start, but they don't know the first steps to take. You'll find out how to get an idea for a business. But let's clarify one point before we get started: People are always wondering if this is a good time to start their business idea. The truth is, there's never really a bad time for starting a business. It's clear that jumping into strong economic times is wise. People have money and try ways to spend it.

Instead, you face three alternatives; starting your own business from scratch, purchasing an existing business, or buying a franchise. They have their own advantages and drawbacks, which will be discussed further.

Developing Your Own Business

One of the most powerful ways to take control of your life and make extra money month after month is to develop your own business. With just a few hours a week, you can start your own business on the side, and no experience even if you have a full-time job. Perhaps best of all, you will be able to choose your hours, choose things you find exciting, perhaps meet people of interest. And it's hard not to get started. The steps you'll take are as follows:

Step 1: Seek a business Idea

People probably find this area the most overwhelming. Perhaps, the most common reason people have not started a business on the side is that they "just don't have a good business idea." But, this is only a mental barrier that you can easily overcome if you look at one area: your strengths. To find a solid business idea, here are four questions you can ask yourself:

1. What qualifications do you have? Now, what do you know and what do you think? The skills and knowledge you have acquired are these.

2. Which friends do you say you're great at?

Give your family and friends a message on Facebook, or ask them IRL: What's great about me? Examples: Workout routines, relationship advice, great sense of fashion, etc.

Step 2: find Top-Paid Customers

Finding customers doesn't have to be a cold calling / emailing nightmare. You just have to remember that the overwhelming majority of your competition is absolutely awful.

Step 3: Pitch Them in Your Work

Speaking directly to their needs is the key to reaching out to potential clients and clients. It is fundamental to human psychology. Imagine that you are on a first date and that's what THEY want and THEIR needs all the other person can talk about. Within minutes you will be sneaking out the window of the bathroom. But imagine if they were asking you questions about you and really seemed interested in your life and problems. A second date would interest you a lot more, wouldn't you? The same is true of pitching yourself to a customer. You need to design your initial reach out to your needs and concerns.

Step 4: Tune the perfect Price

For every beginner, the Price is confusing. And it's full of questions like, "is it too much $ XX/hour? Is it too small?" or "Do I have to charge an hour or a project?" There are no hard-set rates rules, but you can use a few handy thumb rules to find one that works for you.

1. **Drop Three Zeros Method:** Just take your ideal wage, drop three zeros out of it, and voila, you've got your hourly rate. Say you would really like to make at least $40,000, for example. Just take the three zeros out of the finish, and you've got your rate now: $40/hr.

2. **Double your "resentment number":** this is really interesting as well as effective. Ask yourself: What is the lowest rate that you will be working for that will make you resentful about your work? Say you're going to be working at the VERY LEAST for $15/hour. Just double that number, so now you're going to earn $30/hour.

3. **Do what the next guy does:** This method is incredibly straightforward: go to Google and look for the average hourly rate for whatever service you provide. Once you bill your clients, you will get a good sense of where to proceed.

Simply choose one of the above methods and use it as your first option. Once you start charging your customers, you will get a good idea if that's enough for you.

Buying an Existing Business

Buying a business is a big decision but when you pull the trigger to buy an existing business, you get the chance to become an entrepreneur without starting a business from scratch completely. More than 500,000 businesses change hands every year, and that number is expected to skyrocket in the next few years as millions of baby boomers begin to retire and sell their businesses.

It is so popular to buy an existing business because it allows you to skip past some of the pain points and costs of starting a new business. But it can be a long and complicated process from finding a company for sale to closing the contract. Before you start the journey of buying your own business, find out all you need to know to avoid the remorse of the buyer.

Before Buying a Business, Find out Why the Small Business is actually for Sale

Do not just take the word for that from the seller. Certainly, people retire or get sick, but the real reason may be anything from a big-box retailer moving into town and taking customers away to lose a lucrative, traffic-driving contract, like being a post office. Discover the true reason(s) the company is for sale by talking to people who are familiar with the business history you're thinking about buying, such as local realtors, other business people, the local chamber of commerce, and suppliers.

If the business resides in a mall, discuss mall management, lease rates, anchor tenants, etc., with other business owners in the mall.

Ask out what's included in the Price

Figure out what's really available for sale and what market valuation tool is used. If you are buying a small business, what assets do you actually get? People who sell businesses have often prepared a spec sheet, listing the assets involved, and estimating their value. If anything is unclear, ask for details. Pay special attention to any intangible assets, such as goodwill that may be listed. Sellers tend to inflate this value, perhaps thinking about the potential future value of their reputation and the customer base they have established.

Look Into the Arrangement

There is a boy who purchased a good-looking car just to find out he couldn't drive it away because he didn't have a motor?

It's just funny when someone else comes across it. Before you buy a small business, make sure you do your due diligence.

Study the past financial performance of the enterprise. Ask for and review the company's financial statements for the last three years, and consider enlisting the assistance of an experienced CPA to help. You'll also want to know who got the financial data prepared and checked. Was the final version prepared, for example, by the enterprise's internal management and accounting team or by an external accountant?

If the company uses an external accountant, the financial statements should be accompanied by documents that will explain the profundity of the accountant review. An Auditor's Report certifies that there has been a full review, while a Review Engagement Report will present the findings of a limited business review. A Notice to Reader indicates that the accountant prepared the financial statements without carrying out any checks, based on the information given by the company.

Find Out What's Really Worth

Find out what you actually should pay for the business. Using a few different business valuation methods to arrive at a price, is common. This provides a way to arrive at the value from different angles and typically leads to a value range rather than a set figure.

Find Out the Real Value of Business

The real value of the business depends on the revenue generated by the company, and how well it manages its sales and expenses. Examining the financial records of the business should give you a precise, or at least informative, picture of the gross revenues, costs, and profit of the business. Look for buying a business based on the return on investment, not the Price stated. In other words, what you are actually buying is the annual profit, and you are searching for lost revenue opportunities, costs that could be reduced, and other ways to run the business more efficiently than its current owner has done. If you have trouble feeling secure about what the company you want to buy is really worth, ask a professional business appraiser for advice and valuation support.

Take it for a spin

Receive an inside perspective by seeking permission from the seller to wait several days before you buy a business. That isn't necessarily a bad sign if he or she disagrees with that. He doesn't know if you are only posing as a potential buyer to steal confidential business information.

Investigate Your Financing Alternatives

Just like when you buy a car, you need to see if you can actually afford to buy a business. You don't have cash in your hand; then it's time to see who's interested in financing the business you're buying and how much it will cost to fund.

You might find that said traditional lending institutions are more friendly than usual, since financing an established business is generally considered less risky than financing a startup.

You might also want to consider asking the seller to finance a portion of your business purchase. Make an offer Assuming that after your review, you have not found any glaring issues with the company, and you still want to buy the business; it's time to make an offer and start negotiating. You make an offer, and you make a counter-offer to the seller. You two are going to go through a process that will ideally see you meet on middle ground.

If you are asked to accompany your offer to buy a business with a non-refundable deposit, don't be surprised; sellers are typically only interested in dealing with serious buyers. The usual rules of procedure apply. Always be prepared to walk away and not get so caught up in the process that you're pulled past the Price you're actually prepared to pay.

Get a Purchase / Sale Agreement Draw Up

Once you and the seller have reached agreement on the terms and conditions, the specifics must be stated in a contract. Because the contract has to explain any part of the transaction, an attorney will draw up it.

Careful Is Key

Do not be afraid to buy a business that someone else has started and is growing. So long as you resist the temptation to get drawn in by a shiny paint job and do more than just kick the tires before you make an offer.

Buying a Franchise of a small business

When purchasing an existing business doesn't sound right to you, but from scratch, it sounds a bit daunting, you might be suitable for franchise ownership. What is a franchise, and if you're in the right position for one, how do you know? In essence, a franchisee pays an initial fee to a franchisor and a continuing royalty. In return, the franchisee acquires the use of a trademark, the ongoing support of the franchisor, and the right to use the business management system of the franchisor and to sell its products or services.

Apart from a well-known brand name, buying a franchise provides many other benefits that the entrepreneur who starts a business from scratch can't get. Maybe the most important thing is that you get a proven operating system and training on how to use it. New franchisees can typically avoid many of the errors startup entrepreneurs make because the franchisor has already perfected daily operations through trial and error.

Before selling a new outlet, reputable franchisors conduct market research so you'll feel more confident there's a demand for the product or service. Failure to do adequate market research is typically one of the biggest mistakes independent entrepreneurs make; it's done for you as a franchisor. The franchisor also provides you with a clear picture of the competition and how you can stand out from it. Franchisees are finally enjoying the strength of numbers. Many vendors will not manage new businesses or refuse your company because your account is not big enough.

Business Opportunity or franchise?

Essentially, a business opportunity is any bundle of goods or services that encourages the buyer to start a business and, in which the seller portrays that it will provide a marketing or sales strategy, that there is a demand for the product or service, and that the venture will be profitable. Here are other key factors:

• The seller's trademark generally does not feature a business opportunity; buyers operate under his own name.

• Opportunities for businesses tend to be less expensive than franchises and generally do not charge royalty fees ongoing.

• Business opportunities allow buyers to continue without restrictions regarding the geographical market and operations.

• Most business opportunities ventures have no continuing supportive relationship between seller and buyer; buyers are on their own after the initial package is sold.

Advantages

Franchising's greatest strength lies in its ability to bring together independent retailers using a single business model and name. There are many advantages to this affiliation: brand recognition, uniformity in meeting client standards, shared promotional power, and productivity purchasing party.

There are several advantages to franchising for the individual proprietor. The ever-present risk of business failure is minimized when the business plan has already proven successful on the marketplace; the use of an existing brand saves the business owner the cost of creating and promoting a name that consumers can recognize, and the advantages of community advertising and buying make operations more profitable. Additionally, ongoing training creates instant operational expertise that would otherwise have to be acquired through trial and error. Expansion appears to come more naturally with franchising, too. Operating a successful franchise will easily lead to the creation of a second, and then a third, and so on. Fortunes were built in this manner.

Benefits

- Risk reduction
- Turnkey operation
- Standardized products and systems
- Standardized financial and accounting systems
- Collective purchasing power
- Supervision and consulting readily available
- National and local advertising programs
- Point-of-sale advertising
- Uniform packaging
- Continuous R&D
- Financial assistance
- Site selection guidance
- Operations manager

Know also that some franchising systems are better than others. A bad franchise system will not prepare you well to deal with the business's challenges, will not do a good job of helping you when problems arise, and will not make the best use of your advertising dollars.

The Downside

- Loss of control
- A binding contract
- Problems with the franchisor are also your issues

While franchising is designed to bring people into the business who have never previously owned a business, proprietary excitement can create an impulse for progress without proper planning. If you rush to buy a franchise headlong with the expectation of boosting your current working salary, but the earnings don't allow you to pull out more than half of your former salary, you'll be one unhappy camper. Work with a good CPA before you take the plunge to prepare a cash-flow projection for the business.

1.3 Financing Your Small Business

Although they vary in acquiring difficulties, the variety of services available today means that it is more than possible to finance your dream. While most people think of standard bank loans, the fact is there are hundreds of other ways — most of which are more beneficial than a traditional bank loan. Let's explore some of those different funding options to give you a better sense of what opportunities there are.

1. Traditional bank loans

A bank loan is one of the first places most entrepreneurs start. This is called the conventional funding path, which includes setting up a meeting with local banks — preferably those you are already doing business with — and talking to them about their lending practices for small businesses. If a bank offers small business lending options, they will ask you to fill in the application for a loan. This process can take from start to finish, from a couple of weeks to two or three months, anywhere. When time is the key, the first time around should be your goal to be as diligent as possible.

Don't get worked up about the details for those who have never filled in a business loan application. Most loan applications will begin by asking you for basic business information, legal structure, type of business that you are running, what products and services you are selling, etc. You will also be asked to obtain plenty of financial information and confirmation that you are in good standing with the State Secretary (you are paying taxes).

Alas, traditional bank loans are just not as realistic as they once were. Many companies are still wary of giving small businesses money — especially brand new businesses. Business owners also experience some downsides, as interest rates and requirements may be higher than other alternative options.

2. Self-financing

Never write off the self-financing option. This is actually a popular funding approach for startups and is a good place to start. These all play a part in your self-financing capacity. The most popular choice for those pursuing self-financing is to get a home equity loan on the portion of the mortgage that has already been paid out.

In this case, your bank will make a lump-sum loan payment or will extend a credit line based on that amount. The great thing about these credit lines is that they have relatively low-interest rates, and all interest paid on these loans — up to $100,000 — is deductible from taxation. The risk, obviously, is that if you can't repay the debt, you could lose your home. Some options for self-financing include investing against your 401(k) pension plan or using the funds in an IRA.

3. Alternative Small Business Loan

With many banks unwilling or unable to extend small business loans, alternative small business loans might need to be looked into. The beauty of alternative loans is that they are backed by private firms that can make decisions independently of other organizations. Although you may not be able to secure a million-dollar loan, there are many options that range from a few thousand dollars to as much as a quarter of a million dollars. Flexibility is the primary benefit of those loans. Some lenders place tight restrictions on loans, which impedes the ability of a company to use the cash when it is needed. Alternate lenders take a more personal approach, allowing for a smoother experience at times.

4. Crowdfunding

Maybe it didn't seem practical five or six years ago, but crowdfunding is actually a very popular form of financing on the market today. And while traction-gaining through crowdfunding is difficult for most businesses — especially if your products and services aren't sexy and millennial-friendly — the potential benefits are enormous. Websites such as Kickstarter let you launch a campaign, set a funding goal, and offer small incentives to those who donate. The best piece on crowdfunding? All of the money is yours. You don't have to give out equity, or even pay back the money. However, there's a whole science to raise money through crowdfunding sites.

5. Consumer Presales

One of the most ignored funding methods includes the selling of goods before starting your company. This is referred to as the funding of drug presale and can be achieved in some cases. However, the product must be fully developed. Trying to presale products that are not ready for the market can be dangerous for the brand's future. Bitola, a company that sells breastfeeding products, is a perfect example of drug presale funding practicability. In a matter of two weeks, the company was able to collect $50,000 before the actual start of the business. This $50,000 went immediately back into the business, raising the company's value and eliminating the need to take on debt.

6. Friends and Family Members

While most people say that combining your personal life with your business life is a bad idea, friends and family members are often a versatile and easy fundraising choice. Five percent of American adults have provided funding in the past three years to someone starting a business, according to one poll. Very frequently, people spread support to a friend or acquaintance, close family member, parent, or colleague at work. If you decide to ask for funding from friends and family members, it is important to have a strategy and avoid putting pressure on them.

Explore All Your Options

The problem for many business owners and businessmen is that they do not find all of their options. They hone in on a single funding option and spend all their time and energy trying to get that method working. You can increase your chances of securing favorable financing by opening your eyes to all of the above options–and it should be noted that many more exist.

1.4 Determining Feasibility of a Small Business

Before investing too much time and money in a business idea, make sure to assess if it is viable. It is important to be clear how much money you will need to earn to cover your bills, keep future workers working, and provide an appropriate wage for you.

Sure That There's Demand for What You're Offering

Potential demand is critical to whether or not your business is feasible. Is there enough competition today? And if not, in time, you can build demand? Carry out some market research, either through online research or by setting up target customer focus groups.

Do You Have a Market?

Do you know who is going to buy what you want to offer? Your business success might be measured by what motivates your target market to buy your products and services. You will need to make sure the products or services cater to your segment of the target market.

Know your competitors

The next step is to check your likely competitors. Figure out what their respective competitive advantages are, and look at their marketing and pricing policy.

It is a good start to look at their web sites and printed advertising material. You can also search if they have accounts on social media to find out how they are handling themselves and promoting themselves online.

Examine the Numbers

What's it going to take to start your business and then keep it running? How long will it take for your sales to build up to a point where your business can break even and make a profit? To try to answer these questions now requires a few numbers to be projected, which should give you some estimates and a good sense of what it takes to make your business viable over time. Run a cash flow forecast to determine the startup costs and calculate your break-even point to project your idea's viability. In the end, your business should earn you more return than if you put your original investment into a deposit certificate.

Determine Your Price

Find out what market you are offering and what Price customers might be prepared to pay for. Take into consideration the costs of producing and delivering the goods or services, then choose a few quality scenarios. For example, if you're a café deciding how much to charge for coffee, you could come up with three market-based figures:

- $4.50 for a quality coffee with a higher profit margin
- $3.00 which is approximately the Price of local market rivals
- $2.70 to weaken the competition and hopefully gain more customers.

The best Price is usually a combination of customer expectations, or Pricing solutions may need to be checked before you find what works for you.

Cash-Savvy

Having a healthy cash flow is crucial for your business. It helps ensure that you can cover operating costs–and at a crucial time, avoid a money crunch. Working capital is a critical ingredient until it becomes profitable to fund your business. Look at other ways that you can fund money, for example, leasing. Encouraging your clients to pay forthwith and in cash is a useful approach. You may be able to offer discounts for paying with cash or prompt payment discounts to encourage cash payments.

Evite is allowing new clients to extend their terms of credit. Verify that you check their references and have systems in place to quickly track overdue debts.

Have a chat with your accountant or bank manager to make sure your loan portfolio is safe. Short-term loans can fund assets with a short lifespan, whereas long-lived ones require long-term financing. By doing some research to check your idea's feasibility, it helps get it grounded, give you realistic expectations, and better ensure success. Crunching the numbers and assessing market opportunities are good indicators of your idea's business potential. But, keep in mind that some creative thinking might take on new ideas to make them work. We recommend talking with other business owners, a small business specialist, or a mentor.

1.5 How to Promote Your Small Business?

The promotion of business is to run a successful business. It may not in itself be an exciting task, but you just have to! You should spend at least one hour a day promoting your business or planning how to promote it. Promotion needn't be costly. Here are inexpensive ways to promote your business; most of these will cost you a little bit of time.

1. Promote Your Business Whenever You Communicate

You have business cards, but in the course of doing business, you also put out a lot of other documents. Check these to ensure you are taking full advantage of their promotional possibilities.

Is there your business name, motto, contact details (including web address), and slogan on all your correspondence? Any document you send out (whether electronic or printed) should have a letterhead with all of the information about your company.

And don't forget to make sure your email has a full signature that includes all the information about your business and a promotional tagline. You can also add links to a section for Facebook, LinkedIn, Twitter, and Pinterest so that the recipient can connect to you on social media.

Electronic records, such as email, are easy to update with your new business promotion details, whether it's a special offer on your product or service or to let people know that your company has won an award. Remember, it is not just an email; it is a promotional tool for business. Anyway, you send it out, so why not make it work for you?

2. Turn Your Vehicle To a Mobile Billboard

With a vehicle, promotion is not just for White Delivery Vans. Most vehicles have a business name and telephone number, which decorates one of the windows or doors. Think of all the people you see when you drive around your vehicle. Wraps are printed digitally on a specially applied media, and will not harm the paint job of the vehicle. According to the American Outdoor Advertising Association, a single vehicle wrap can generate 30.000 to 70.000 views per day depending on your location and population size, making it one of the most inexpensive ways to promote your business. And if you want to go out all over, there's nothing like an eye-catching advertising special paint job.

3. Use Social Media to Promote Your Business

Facebook, Twitter, and YouTube are great ways for social media to promote your business. Recently, when we had a power outage that impacted certain parts of our city, a good example of how this can be successful was highlighted to me. On Facebook, one of the local restaurants posted that they had power and were open to business and packed with customers in an hour. Create a social media strategy to get social media going. You can film and post video advertisements for your products or services on YouTube if you are able to take video (or know someone who's).

4. Promote Your Business by Internet

Don't forget to write articles when you're considering how to promote your business. Well-written articles can make free advertising available and create positive word-of-mouth. For example, if you're a realtor, you could write a piece about making your home ready for the show. If you are a website designer, you may be able to write a piece about evaluating the usability of the website. Where to go? Since the aim is to promote your business, ideally, you would like it to appear in a publication that will be reading your target market.

- **Blogs/websites:** Astronomical numbers of those hungry for information exist. Putting one or more of your posts on a site that gets little traffic will not benefit you and may even damage your business if it is a site that looks Sammy. You must also make careful choices regarding the target market. If you're selling baby clothes, many (if any) of the customers you're hoping to impress will not get one of your articles published on a blog about Search Engine Optimization. Getting your work on a popular blog that is directly related to baby raising would be a much better fit.

- **Magazines:** The magazine industry is not yet dead, and many are also always searching for material. It must be published in which it is likely to be read by your target market. Even freelance writing sites provide a lot of information about all sorts of magazines that could publish your efforts.

- **Newspapers:** It is also a really good option to put an article about your business promotion. Try to contact your local paper Business Editor and pitch your article. If this approach fails, you may be able to get your piece into the paper's printed or online version by sending it to the Editorial section as a letter.

5. Use Buddy Marketing (Cross-Promotion)

Buddy marketing involves joining another business and pooling your resources to promote all of your business. If you send out brochures, for example, you might include a leaflet and/or business card from another company that has agreed to do the same for you. That gives you the opportunity to reach a whole new pool of potential clients.

In addition, you could plan and carry out business promotions with additional businesses. For example, a pet store and a pet grooming business could use joint ads, or run a contest together. This can significantly reduce the cost of promoting your business and allow each business to employ promotional techniques that would be too expensive to implement on their own.

In the next chapter, you will learn how to run running Small Business.

Chapter 02: Running a Small Successful Business

Most people fear to start their own company because they don't know how to run a small business. It takes more than pure hard work to run a small business. It's important to have a basic knowledge of the management of a company and an overall understanding of the services that you give to your clients. If you do have these things, it can be rewarding to run a business, particularly when you provide a good or service that you can stand behind. With a little planning, you can trustfully start your own business.

A small business has many avenues to be productive, from financial returns to work-life balance to making the world a better place. To run a successful small business, you first need to develop a clear idea of what you see as success. Keep this vision in mind as you work out the mechanics of running your business, and make choices that will advance you along this path. Whether or not your primary goal in running a business is to earn a great deal of money, you have to make enough to keep your business afloat. To be financially sustainable, a small business needs to earn more income than basic operating expenses. Even if you are not familiar with business bookkeeping and confident with it, you should learn practical skills to help you understand what's going on with your business financials.

- **Financing Your Small Business:** Unless you run a solo business from a home computer that you already own, you'll probably need some financing to start your business as well as regular infusions during slow periods or when your business is growing. Cultivate capital sources, such as friends and family, and develop relationships with banks. Assess your own financial risk capacity. There are no right or wrong answers as to the right amount of capital to put up, but if you have a clear sense of how much you're willing to invest, and how you're going to regroup financially if things aren't going as planned, you'll be well-positioned. Develop a plan to repay what you are borrowing. Set out a timetable, and consider how much your business needs to earn to make this plan a success.

- **Keeping it Legal:** Do your homework, so you know how to legally start and operate your business. This process will initially take some extra time, but in the long run, it is likely to save you time. Get all the licenses you need to run a business in your town and country, as well as any permits you may need for your particular industry. Choose a business structure that makes sense for your own relationship, such as a partnership, if you start with a friend. Consult with an attorney about the best structure for your specific circumstances. Follow the business's rules and regulations and pay your taxes on time.

- **Quality of Life:** There are laws against workplace exploitation, but there are no laws against self-misconduct. Most small business owners work grueling hours and struggle to find a balance between work and life.

- **Know Your Boundaries:** Comprehend how much you're willing to work to keep your business successful and where you're likely to draw the line. Your willingness and ability may change over time as if you're emotionally willing to work every waking hour for the first year you're in business, but expect to take regular holidays once your business is established.

- **Clearly Communicate:** how your business will affect your home life with your loved ones. Understand their level of tolerance and understanding, and, if necessary, enlist additional help such as child care for your family or additional employees for your business.

There are also many things you need to learn in detail in this chapter which is as follows:

2.1 Business Planning: Key to Success

No matter how big your business and in which industry you are, every business needs a successful business plan in order to be successful. There's an old saying that "failing to prepare is planning to fail" — and yet many new business owners are attempting to just wing it out without even going through the process of writing a business plan outline or setting any clear business goals.

Don't allow your business to have that happen. Running a business is complex and multifaceted, and you need to get a sense of what your business is all about, how you will make money and how you will manage your business and grow for the future. Ideally, your business plan will serve as a road map and "living document," which you can update and refer back to when making future decisions. And if you have a live copy even better "in the cloud," then you can easily access it and refresh it when there is something to it.

Business plan Small Business Outline Here are a few key items to be included when designing a business plan for your LLC or Corporation:

1. Mission Statement

What is your company doing; what is the intention of your business, and what is the difference in the world that your business does make? Many people assume that the mission statements are for large corporations only, or that a mission statement must be boring and stuffy. But it's not true! Even the smallest companies can take some time to sit down and write out exactly what your business is doing and why it exists. This can help to clarify your thinking for the remaining outline of your business plan.

2. Business Model

How does it make money for your business? Does your business sell to consumers (B2C) or other (B2B) companies? How are you going to price out your products or services? What is your average margin of profit on each sale? Will you be marketing those goods as "loss leaders" to make bigger profits from the more profitable items in your stock?

3. Target Markets

Who are the right clients for you? When you market to buyers, what are your main demographics for customers in terms of age, employment, place, and lifestyle? When you sell to companies, what are your customers' ideal criteria— the type of company, the size of the market, and the typical business problems you are helping them solve? Spend some time thinking about how to understand and get inside your target clients' heads.

4. Marketing Plan

Make a plan for how to reach them now that you know "who" you want to reach. How will you spread the word about your company and be able to connect with potential clients? There are many different marketing strategies and tactics, ranging from marketing with search engines and targeted Facebook ads to traditional methods such as direct mail and brochures. Take examples of what other companies in your industry are doing to reach customers, and emulate those methods

5. Business Goals

Where would you like to have your business in five years? Do you expect some revenue targets or expanded hiring to help your business grow? What are the milestones you are going to use to measure that progress?

6. Location

Where do you operate your business, and where do you wish to operate? Want to run a local small business or operate in multiple towns, regions, or countries? Does this require multiple offices or regular business travel if you want to expand into selling products or offering services at multiple locations? Make a map of where you want to get your business going.

7. Financing

Will you use your business plan to raise money from investors or to secure a company loan? If so, you'll need a detailed financial plan for how much money you need and how you'll be using the money, and how you can repay the loan or help your investors make a return on their investments. Financing can be complex, time-consuming, and may require you to relinquish some control over your business to investors who would expect to have a say on business strategy and operation.

8. Operations

Give some thought to the day-to-day running of your business overall. How are you going to work with the suppliers and vendors? What workspace or retail space, or storage space for warehouse/inventory? How are your products going to get from one place to another-what are your shipping and logistics plans? Use your business plan to map a picture of how your company's "work" is done.

9. Employee Recruitment

What is your plan to hire employees? How many employees do you expect to hire, and what will they do within the first year? What functions do you want to handle your business yourself (sales, technical support, product design, etc.), and what functions do you want to hire for immediately? If you are not ready to hire full-time employees, may you recruit freelancers and independent contractors to help upgrade your business?

10. Lifestyle Design

Ultimately, your successful business plan is not just about "business" but about your life. Your business needs to support the overall purposes of your life. What hours do you want to work, for example, and how many holiday days would you like to take each year? How do you get out of business when you need to? Can you work in your business remotely, or do you have to be "there" every day and be on-site? Aside from the financial aspects, what is your personal definition of "success" for your business and life? Want to be able to live as a "digital nomad" and work remotely? You may not attain all of your lifestyle goals, especially in the hectic early stages of building your business. But it's worth spending time visualizing exactly how you want your life to look like a successful business owner.

Why Should You Write a Business Plan?

The business plan for your company is a blueprint. It's equally risky to start a business without a business plan. It's not a static business. They sometimes make the mistake of thinking of a business plan as a single document that you simply put together and then set aside when you start. There's something to check the to-dodo list out and do with. But in reality, the business plan for any business will change over time as the business develops, and as its objectives change, any particular business may have multiple business plans.

If you are not yet convinced, here are five valid reasons to write a strategic plan before starting a new business.

1. To Test Your business Idea to Be Viable

Writing a business plan is the best way, other than to go out and do it, to test whether an idea is feasible to start a business. The business plan, in that sense, is your safety net. If working through a business plan reveals your business idea is untenable, you'll be saved a lot of time and money.

At the marketing research or competitive analysis point, an idea for starting a business is often discarded, allowing you to move on to a new (and better) concept.

Sadly, many potential business owners are persuaded that their concept for a product or service is a project that they can't ignore, so they don't take the time to do the homework they need and work through a business plan. The more you know about your market, prospective customers, and competition, the greater the probability of success for your company.

2. To Give Your New Business the Best Chance of Success

Writing a business plan will ensure that you pay attention to your new business' broad operational and financial goals and the small details, such as budgeting and market planning. Ultimately, the process will make for a smoother startup period and fewer unforeseen issues as your business get up and running.

Budgeting and market planning will help you define your target market, your unique selling proposal, optimum pricing strategies, and outline how you intend to sell and deliver your products to clients. In addition, creating an implementation budget will help determine the criteria for development and operating capital.

3. To Raise Funding

In order to get off the ground, most new businesses require start-up and operating capital. Without a well-developed business plan, there is no chance of angel investors obtaining debt financing from established financial institutions such as banks or equity financing. Established businesses also often need money to do things like buying new equipment or real estate, or downturns in the market. Getting an up-to-date business plan gives you a much better chance to get the money you need to continue to operate or grow. Investors and financiers are always looking at the risk of default, and word of mouth in a properly prepared business plan is no replacement for written facts and figures.

4. Making Business Planning Manageable and Efficient

If you plan to start a business, a business plan is essential, but it is also an important tool for established businesses. Viable businesses are dynamic, evolving, and rising. The original business plan for your organization, when you set new goals, needs to be reviewed. Reviewing the business plan may also help you see what goals have been achieved, what changes need to be made, or what new ways to grow your business.

5. To Attract Investors

Whether you want to venture capitalists to shop your business or to attract angel investors, you need a solid business plan. A presentation may pique their interest, but they will need a well-written document they can study before they are prepared to commit to any investment. Be prepared to scrutinize your business plan. All venture capitalists and angel investors will want to carry out extensive background checks. If your business does not have one, perhaps it's time to start writing it. A business plan writing process can do wonders to explain where you have been and where you are going.

2.2 Outsourcing

Describe outsourcing as delegating services that you don't want to do, or have no time to do, to someone outside the business (not an employee) who typically can do them better and faster. Outsourcing is a buzzword that, in the past decade, has arisen more, but the definition itself is not fresh. For many years, businesses have been outsourcing, in one form or another. In the section which follows, we outline the basics.

Which jobs are outsourced?

Look at this list of most commonly outsourced Small Business functions:

A. Accounting and bookkeeping

Accounting (the start-to-end process of collecting financial data, generating financial statements, and preparing tax forms) and bookkeeping (only the collection-of-financial-data function) provide a range of opportunities for outsourcing. You can hire someone to do all of your accounting and bookkeeping, for example, or you can hire someone to do just your payroll, just your financial statements, or just your tax returns. Because the average entrepreneur typically does not have a good knowledge of accounting and bookkeeping skills, our advice here is that these roles should be among the first you consider outsourcing.

B. Human Resources

The various human resource roles should be next in line for outsourcing consideration as the company grows. Human resources include a wide range of non-product, known-customer, and non-customer-related issues, such as

- New employee hiring practices
- Employee policy and procedures manuals
- Payroll and related information collection systems
- Employee training on human resources issue

- Employee training on a wide range of awareness issues, such as ethics and sexual harassment.

C. Manufacturing

For most goods, the manufacturing process is costly, time-consuming, and extremely thorough. The outsourcing of the manufacturing role makes much sense for many entrepreneurs, particularly the innovative and/or sales types that usually gravitate to this profession. Even if your core business is manufacturing, certain elements of your product may lend themselves to subcontractors outsourcing their fabrication.

D. Sales

Outsourcing sales is certainly the most potentially hazardous of outsourcing options but one that is used by some businesses, including those employing reps from manufacturers. We say "potentially hazardous" because it is difficult to impart to outsiders the enthusiasm and knowledge necessary to sell the product or service of your business most effectively. Sales are definitely the last of the tasks to consider outsourcing, although doing so works well for some small companies.

Finding Out What to Outsource

Here's the question: How do you decide which services are to be outsourced and which are to be maintained internally? Of course, each business and owner is different, but you have to answer those questions before you make the decision:

> Could I handle my current cash better if I outsource it? Above all, the answer here will depend on how much cash you have. For example, by outsourcing the manufacturing process, you reduce the costs associated with keeping a raw materials inventory and recruiting manufacturing workers. Or, by outsourcing your sales roles, you reduce the costs of keeping a sales force in place.

- What should I do best? Because your time is finite, why spend a lot of time doing things that you're not doing well (such as bookkeeping) when you can farm out those duties, leaving you more time to do the things you're doing, right?
- Will the cost of outsourcing tasks include a product (service) that is of better quality than what I can produce at the same cost? The best sources of outsourcing are almost always experts in their areas of expertise. You should not, of course, outsource yourself until you find a competent specialist.
- How do I like to do most? We can guarantee this: If you choose to keep your bookkeeping or human resource functions in-house, you will end up spending no small amount of time on issues related to those functions over the years. Think about it: Do you want to spend your time in this way?

In the end, the decision whether to outsource will be based primarily on what you enjoy doing.

2.3 Simplifying Your Accounting

If that were a perfect world, you wouldn't need a system of accounting. You'd just let your business checkbook do the talk. You would pay your bills and deposit your receipts, and anything left over at year-end would represent your profit. How simple (and cheap) a procedure like that would be. When weighing one of your assets (cash), does your checkbook talk. In addition, your checkbook only measures the cash of today; it does not give you the foggiest idea of what will be the cash balance of tomorrow or the next month. Will you have enough cash in the bank to pay the bills for the month, meet the payroll next Friday, or pay the quarterly tax payments due in 30 days? Who says what? Not talking about the check-book.

The problem is that the checkbook for your business can't do anything like this:

- Keep score (on anything other than cash)
- Provide the percentages and ratios you need to help you handle your business.
- Provide you with the trends to determine your business direction
- Present the information you need to evaluate your business, like it or not; accounting is one of the most important business functions.

Whether you intend to outsource your accounting eventually or do all the work yourself, accounting demands your undivided attention at the startup stage. The mistake we see in the start-up stage is that entrepreneurs do not learn the basics of accounting and how they apply to the business. Learn the basics early, or you are never going to take the time.

Introduction of Some Common Systems

When determining which accounting system to use, you have three options to consider:

- Accounting services outsourcing (this decision is to be made before the doors open for your business)
- A manual in-house bookkeeping system
- An in-house computer-based accounting system it follows a discussion about the manual and computer-based options.

1. Manual Bookkeeping Systems

Maintaining a manual bookkeeping system is definitely the fastest and easiest of the two options in-house. Visit your local office-supply store, buy one of the many manual bookkeeping ledger systems and journals.

You won't have to buy an expensive computer or the software to go with it; the only accessories you need are a #2 pencil or pen and no small amount of your (or someone else's) time depending on the complexity of your business. Aside from the low cost of a manual bookkeeping system, another advantage of such a system is that you are learning from the ground up the basics of standard double-entry accounting systems-a skill that will keep you in good stead as your business grows.

The downside of the manual-entry system is that it can be extremely time-consuming, especially when your business has a lot of activity, and time is money in the small business world. Additionally, the information you manually gather will not always provide you with the profundity of financial data you need to make important business decisions. Manual bookkeeping is, finally, more prone to human error than computer-based systems.

Follow the step-by-step instructions inside the ledgers and journals to perform a relatively uncomplicated, connect-the-dots bookkeeping process after you purchase your manual system. Create the entries in the general journal pages during your fiscal year (the papers are where you create the entries; the ledgers are where you complete the entries for the journals).

The manual program that you are buying provides descriptions for each of the following categories along with examples:

- Your disbursements, by category of expenses and/or capital accounts.
- Your business receipts (earnings).
- Specific period-end adjustment entries intended to document items such as depreciation, deferred taxes, and accumulated payroll.

Fill in your journal entries at the end of the year, summarizing the activity of the year. Instead, if you choose, you should hand your papers over to a tax advisor or certified public accountant (CPA), wait a few weeks, and be presented with a written statement of profit and loss, a balance sheet, and the amount owed for your year-end tax payment. On the other hand, if you are that special entrepreneur who actually enjoys the bookkeeping process, you can expand the manual bookkeeping process to include the year-end preparation of your statement of profit and loss, as well as the balance sheet, leaving only your taxes to be calculated by a tax practitioner.

Finally, in those cases where your business is a relatively uncomplicated sole proprietorship or partnership, you may be determined by the preparation to carry out the manual process. When it comes to how much of your own bookkeeping and taxes you're doing yourself, your time and patience are the only limitations. The main issue to consider when determining how much of your accounting you should do, or how little of it is how best to use your time.

In addition to the previously described general ledger and journal features, most manual bookkeeping ledger and journal systems also include the forms you need to maintain such subsidiary records as monthly payrolls, accounts receivable schedule, accounts payable schedule, and inventory worksheets (which will be discussed in detail in the upcoming chapters).

2. Computer-based systems

If you have an account payable schedule, Although the least expensive computerized software package available is a tad more expensive than a comparable manual system, if you use it properly, the computerized system should save you time, provide you with more information, and create a basis for you to grow into a more sophisticated system as your business expands (hopefully).

When shopping for your first accounting package, you can consider four categories of computerized systems and remember that the system you ultimately choose should depend on the size and complexity of your business.

2.4 Managing Your Expenses

Imagine a kid after a long Trick-Or-Treating Halloween night. They have gathered a massive loot of sweets, so they need to figure out how and when to eat it when they get home. Will they eat everything at once, or do they conserve it over a long time? They might just eat it on the weekends. It's a big move!

Maybe kids like sweets more than business owners like cash in the bank, but paying bills is definitely much less fun than eating candy, it's a rivalry. Small business owners have to monitor expenses consistently so that they can pay wages, buy inventories, cover rent, etc. In fact, not running out of money is the #1 priority of all the things business owners need to do.

Focusing on revenue and growth is vital, but here's what the best-managed businesses are, but if there's no capital, it won't be achievable. Here's what the best-managed businesses with expenses are:

a. Stay On Top Of It

Set up a regular monitoring process, and even if you, as the owner, don't handle the information directly, it's important that you stay fully informed. Many people do not like the figures, and they are able to outsource them to someone else. But if you don't understand your performance, cash position, payables, etc., you won't know how to make business decisions.

b. Stay Vigilant

Most small businesses, especially brand new ones, must keep "lean and mean" and managing expenses is an integral part of that business mindset. Make a schedule of the costs critical to your business. Using an accounting software program is essential, which will be easy to use and keep up to date. Check those spending areas certainly with a financial professional like your accountant.

c. Personnel Spending Affects Almost Every Business

Even if you're a sole operator, test your compensation expenditure and be practical. Definitely at the outset, keeping staffing expenditures as low as possible with all their associated costs. If you can handle a number of roles yourself as the shareholder, at a later date, you will be able to better gauge the staff requirements. Note, salary is just one payroll expense, and the additional benefits and tax costs can be a burden on a young business. But recruiting part-time workers or contractors will help offset some of the costs at first.

d. Be Vigilant With Overhead Expenses

When you work in a home office room, review the various overheads, including electricity, telephone, and insurance coverage. Investigate new telephone and utility technologies that might be beneficial in keeping costs down. Businesses often feel like having a fancy office makes them feel legit, but a small business owner can avoid expensive office space by using meeting rooms in their local library (often free) or low-cost office space such as "We-Works." Shared office space also reduces the office equipment costs such as fax machines, copiers, and furniture. Generally, fixed costs don't push further business, so it's best to run one as thinly as possible.

e. Beware Inventory

If you start a small business and have to carry inventory, then setting up an inventory system is imperative. Excess inventory will be a burden on any small business, and sparse inventory can hamper sales as well. Really, inventory is just cash sitting on a shelf, so you don't want it to sit too long. Make sure you have a tracking system that you can quickly check-" lost "inventory isn't an expense you'd like to face. Factor in the costs of shipping your items. There are numerous competing freight services, and it pays to compare several and often re-evaluate. Such providers usually raise prices annually, and at high peak shipping times, they will add a fuel surcharge.

f. Cost Marketing is better than Cost-effective Marketing.

Once you're spending money on advertising, that cash goes away forever, whether you're getting customers or not. Word of mouth is the best marketing-your customers love your product so much that they tell their friends. But you can also use other inexpensive resources such as social media for marketing your business, including your local town blogs. Partnerships are another affordable way to find customers, as you can pool resources and use complementary lists of customers to reach new leads. Managing your costs will have a direct impact on your small business profitability. You'll benefit from keeping a firm grip on all costs as you expand and grow.

Tips to Manage Your Expenses of Your Small Business

Also, if you are using a bookkeeper or accountant to do your accounting, it will make the process much easier to maintain your own records and handle your expenses effectively. We will share some of our own ideas on how to handle the expenses in this blog, as well as knowledge gleaned from working with our clients.

1. **Know What Records You Need to Keep Legally For Your Business**

The types of records you need to keep, and how long you need to keep them, depends on the type of entity you are–e.g., sole trader, limited company, etc. –and other factors, such as whether you are registered for VAT. Sales, purchases, payments, receipts, payroll, expenses, and mileage should be included in records. Keeping your bank and card statements, book checks, and book deposit stubs can help with that.

2. **Using Technology to Create the Records**

If you are a small business, it doesn't have to mean having a pricey software package–it can be enough to have a simple excel spreadsheet of costs. Whatever program/software you choose, whether a spending report template in excel or otherwise, digital records will simplify and make your expense management more efficient.

3. **Group Expenses Into Categories**

To keep track of your expenses against your budget, it helps categorize your expenses into departments or groups, such as Office Supplies, Mileage, Stock, Wages, etc. This will enable you to analyze specific categories if you wish and to keep track of the allocation of the majority of your expenditure. However, making sure that you consistently post expenses under the same category is important. Otherwise, any meaningful analysis becomes difficult to do.

4. **Report Your Expenses When You Incur Them**

Reporting your expenses annually is far more effective than storing them all up to the end of the tax year. Take time to make a list once a month or even once a week. This also helps to avoid the 'loss' of the costs you think about.

An additional benefit of doing your expenses regularly is that you can assess any areas where you overspend.

It is a good idea to use a travel expenses report template for mileage claims. This isn't as formal as it sounds–it can be purely a form that records each business journey, including the location' from' and' to' and the number of miles. This can be kept in the car in such a way that details can be recorded at the time, instead of having to be remembered later.

5. Notice Recharges

When you pass on costs to your consumers (known as recharging), it is doubly important that you keep track not only of what was spent but of the customer it should be credited to.

6. Hold Business and Personal Transactions Separate

Whenever possible, it is much better to avoid making business-related purchases using personal accounts, cards, or cash. This makes the accounting process much easier and will help give you a more accurate impression of cash flow, income, and expenditure for the business.

2.5 Developing a Marketing Plan

To ensure focus and direction in your marketing, you'll need to plan ahead of time. The development of a marketing plan will help you set clear goals, but will also give you a clear path to achieving them. Doesn't sound pretty obvious? And yet many companies are missing this move, or making a plan but never going back. This results in a huge amount of time wasted and a lack of momentum, let alone frustration.

Any Marketing Plan?

You'll have more than likely set some goals when you wrote your business plan. Maybe key things that you want to achieve in your business over the coming 6-12 months or beyond.

At least some of those targets are also likely to relate directly to sales and profits. This is where your marketing plan's coming in! Marketing is (or ought to be!) your key strategy when it comes to finding and maintaining customers and thus making revenue.

Yeah, other things like branding and customer service will also play a part in that–but if your customers never find you in the first place, then it doesn't matter how good your branding and service is, they won't see it. What's your marketing plan, then? It's where you break down the ways you'll find new customers, get them to like you, trust you, and, ultimately, buy from you and be loyal to your business. What should your Marketing Plan include?

Your Target Market

As discussed in our article ' Finding New Customers,' understanding who your ideal customers are is absolutely essential to keep your marketing focused and efficient. You may have just one specific type of customer, or you may have a number of different customer persons, but it is important to have as clear a picture as possible of these because it will affect the rest of your marketing strategies.

Your Revenue Streams

How do you plan to make a profit? Maybe you're a hairdresser, so one stream is through your hairdressing service, and another is through hair products you promote and sell to your clients. Or maybe you have a store, and one revenue stream is made from the sales you make in the shop, while another is made from online sales. That stream would require that your marketing plan includes its own marketing strategy. Don't forget to include ALL revenue streams–such as affiliate marketing, website advertising, etc.

It's also useful to include how you get the payment for each of these revenue streams here. Customers will pay in person, for example? Do you want to have an online payment facility? These are the kinds of questions that you need to know. What is your unique point of sale (USP) that will make people choose you over your competitors? Maybe you're better value than anybody else, or your customer service goes beyond and beyond. Maybe your product is unique per se? Whatever makes your company stand out should be part of your marketing and set out in your marketing plan.

Branding

The way you actually brand your business is a part of your marketing. Marketing is all about attracting customers, and branding is shaping what customers feel and think about your business, so the two are aligned very well. If your branding presents your company as high quality and luxury, then your marketing strategy shouldn't tell people what a good value your service is, or how nice it is on a budget for people. You need to align your branding and marketing, so make sure your branding is clearly outlined in your marketing plan.

As with branding, your pricing also has to be aligned with your customer's message. When you tell customers that your goods are of high quality and luxury and your name screams the same, then you need to suit your price. Furthermore, getting the pricing strategy outlined will help form the messaging itself as the price will be a key element of any copy of sales you publish.

Marketing Channels

We laid out a number of different types of marketing in our' Finding new customers ' article.

This is where you need to pin down what you're focusing on for your business.

Many organizations will use a range of platforms, but few, if any, need to use them all. Think about which one will work best to attract and focus on your target market.

Marketing Targets

The goals should be precise and measurable. You could go for something like' Get ten new customers every week' rather than' Get more customers.' Instead of' increasing revenue,' try to' increase revenue over the year by 5 percent.' You see the idea, do you?

As well as the above general marketing goals, which are based on increasing customers and revenues, go a step further and think about how each of your chosen marketing channels will achieve this. Set these goals too. Your blog may be aimed at enhancing your thought leadership. What would that be a good measure of? Maybe the amount of engagement that you get in the form of comments? Or how many new subscribers you get as a consequence of your blog posts? Try to be as specific as possible with what you hope each channel will achieve and how you'll measure success. This will help you stay focused on marketing and not waste any time that is not actually aligned with your marketing goals.

Marketing Strategies

Now that you have stipulated each of your marketing goals, you can plan how to achieve them. This is likely to be broken down by channel and/or revenue stream, once again.

Say, for example, that your business does online crafts making and selling. Perhaps one of your goals would be to increase sales by 10 per week.

You have chosen social media and email as your main channels of marketing for this. So your plan might be to use social advertising to drive people into subscribing to your email list and then use an automated email sequence to tell customers more about you, your business, and your crafts.

Each email could focus on another product and end with a clear call for action as to how the customer can make a purchase if they wish. In the planning phase, the clearer you can be on your strategy, the easier you will find that strategy executed.

Measure & Review

This is that important step! With all the world's planning, nothing actually beats doing it to see what works and what doesn't. By doing this, you can understand and do more of what resonates well, and you can tweak and improve what has not worked so well.

Always think about your goals and how you know if they succeeded. Something like' getting ten new customers a week' is fairly simple to measure. But don't forget to calculate every single step of the process. So, go back to our example of the craft selling business above. They would need to measure how many conversions they got from their social ads, how many people they opened their emails, and how many sales they actually made at the end of the process. That way, if they only sell eight more, they'll have a much clearer picture of why.

They may get a 50 percent conversion on their ads, maybe another 50 percent of people who open the emails buy, but in fact, only 2 percent of people who receive the emails actually open them. This shows very clearly that what needs more focus is the email subject line–perhaps a small tweak here could dramatically improve the results. For each of these metrics in place, the business owner might have wasted valuable time changing their advertisements and emails that worked fine!

2.6 Keeping Customers Loyal

Customer loyalty is a concept that has changed rapidly with technology developments and the shift to mobile customer experience in recent times. We're going to explain how small businesses can cut the noise and develop customer loyalty to keep customers longer.

Is customer loyalty achievable for small businesses, or is the "loyal customer" concept a thing of the past? "Brands" are certainly not quite what they used to be. The mobile revolution has made readily available information for consumers to make more educated buying decisions. Below are some ideas that can help your small business create customer loyalty.

1. Setting Up Ways To Communicate With Your Clients

The frequent communication with your clients keeps you fresh in mind and allows you to pass on important information. Save the time to set up a database containing contact details such as email addresses, mailing addresses, or phone numbers.

Do not forget to throw messages which are either funny or useful reminders.

2. Providing Additional Benefits to Your Most Loyal Customers

One of the simplest–and perhaps one of the easiest–ways to reward customer loyalty is to provide extra benefits to your most reliable customers. Customers love to get a little extra, whether it's the ability to skip the line, special meeting-and-greets, or immediate seating.

3. Consider Various Payment Plans

There are some businesses out there that, during certain times of the year, is very seasonal and run into cash flow problems.

For example, in the summer months, when weddings are in full swing, a wedding shop usually gets most of its sales, but they struggle in the winter. The plan worked because by supplying them with manageable monthly payments, it benefited consumers and supported the company by bringing in cash during a slow year. In reality, customers were so pleased that they also recommended the store to others, and the company saw a nearly 400 percent increase in total revenue.

4. Provide Great Customer Service

While this may seem like a given, it is one tip that bears repeating as it is so important. One survey showed that 51 percent of customers ended their business relationship in 2013 because they were unhappy with the service they received.

Customers remember when they are being treated well, and when they are being treated poorly, they remember. They usually tell their friends and family in either case, and that can mean either more business for you or a loss of business opportunities.

5. Don't Rely Too Much On Technology

In our technologically advanced society, we still want the ability to interact with others, even with text messages and emails. Therefore, it is important to remember that while automated telephone systems can save money, highly trained clients create loyalty.

6. Don't Forget To Smile

A UK study tracked down the words used to greet customers as they entered a shop, and then cross-checked how much they spent in the store.

The terms used to greet customers as they entered a shop were monitored by a UK report, and then cross-checked how much they spent in the store.

The study showed that up to 67 percent of shoppers who were accepted with a welcome and a smile spent more than shoppers who were not welcomed.

7. Give a Reason For Being Loyal To Customers

Many people think Apple has some of the most loyal fans out there. Customers go to great lengths with bumper stickers, tattoos, and vehement arguments in favor of all the products to prove just how much they love the company. Neuroscientists have recently tested Apple fans ' brains and found that when those customers think of their favorite items, the same part of the brain that illuminates when religious people think about their god is triggered. It is impossible to underline just how important customer loyalty is in the business climate of today.

Dealing with Dissatisfied Customers

You can offer the fairest prices and provide great customer service, and you will still end up with the occasional unhappy client. How you deal with complaints-both justified and unjustified-is vital to your business's long-term reputation and health. The following sections contain our time-tested advice to deal with your unhappy and sometimes distressing clients.

Most people like to believe they're awesome listeners. The reality is most are not. And even if you're a good listener, you have moments when you don't listen well for any of a variety of reasons.

From work, family, friends, daily chores, and obligations, you get busy and stressed out by the competing demands on your time. You also have days when you're tired, feeling unwell, or getting bad news or bad experiences.

Another impediment to listening well is that you may be persuaded that an unhappy client is actually a troublemaker.

However, as with all personal relationships, your preconceived notions about others (dare we call them prejudices) can keep you from hearing legitimate and real concerns and reasons to be dissatisfied.

Develop a Solution

When a customer complaints, remember that they are complaining about the deal they received because of their dissatisfaction with it. The next step, following listening to complaints from the customer, is to develop a solution that addresses the complaints.

There are two ways you can come to a solution:

1. You can ask the customer what solution, he or she is going to propose, and then you can see how this compares with what you can do. The advantage of asking the customer for a solution is the same as with any other form of negotiation (which is what happens in this situation after all). If you let the unsatisfied customer make the opening offer, you know exactly where you're standing and what you need to do to satisfy him. Imagine the benefit you can derive when the solution for the client is less expensive than what you were about to offer. In such a circumstance, there is a sudden opportunity for you to take up an unpleasant situation and turn it into an opportunity to reinforce the loyalty of the complaining client to your business.
2. You can propose a solution yourself and then wait for a solution he or she thinks is better to counter the customer with. Only when the customer doesn't have a solution or refuses to come up with it is it time to propose one. Suppose, for example, that you run a professional service business, and you are responsible for missing a customer appointment-either because of a scheduling error or because you are behind schedule, and the customer simply couldn't wait any longer. You quickly find out that the

customer is really angry at having stood up after taking valuable time out of his working day. Your solution could go something like this to ease the unhappiness of the customer:
- Excuse himself for the time he wasted.
- Ask for the solution it recommends.
- Offer a discount if he does not have a solution (maybe 15 or 20 percent off the appointment price when rescheduling).
- When the customer returns for a rescheduled appointment, be completely assured that he is seen on time and that he has provided the best service possible.

Chapter 03: Keeping Your Books

Many new business owners get daunted by the mere idea of accounting and bookkeeping. But in fact, they're both pretty simple. Basic objectives of bookkeeping and accounting share:

- Keep track of your income and expenses, enhancing your chances of making a profit, and
- Collecting the financial information you need to file your various tax returns.

Your records are not required to be kept in any particular way. As long as your records accurately reflect the revenues and expenses of your business, they will be acceptable to the IRS. You can produce your own ledgers and reports, or rely on accounting software, depending on the size of your company and the number of sales.

3.1 How to Keep Your Books?

When broken down into three steps, the actual process of keeping your books is easy to understand.

- ➢ Keep receipts or other acceptable records of each payment to and from your business's expenses.
- ➢ Summarize your income and expense records periodically (daily, weekly, or monthly) on some basis.

Those principles are exactly the same whether you do your accounting by hand on ledger sheets or use accounting software.

Step One: Keeping Your Receipts

Each sale and purchase of your business must be backed up by some kind of record containing the amount, the date, and other relevant information about that sale.

These will be used to create summaries of your transactions. Your method of holding receipts will, from a legal point of view, range from slips stored in a cigar box to a sophisticated cash register hooked into a computer system. In practice, you're going to want to pick a system that fits your business needs. For example, with a bare-bones approach, a small service business that handles only relatively few jobs can get by. But the more your business produces sales and expenditures.

Step Two: Update and Post to Databases

A finalized ledger is nothing but a summary of earnings, expenses, and anything else that you keep track of (entered by group and date from your invoices). Later, you use these overviews to answer specific financial queries about your business, such as whether you make money and, if so, how much. Post the receipts periodically. On a regular basis — like every day, once a week, or at least once a month — the amounts from your sales and purchase receipts should be transferred to your ledger.

Your timeline for posting depends on your sales numbers. In general, the more sales you make, the more frequently you should post to your ledger. For example, a retail store should post daily hundreds of sales, amounting to thousands of dollars each day. It's important to see what happens with that volume of sales every day, and not fall back with the paperwork. To do this, the busy dealer should use a cash register that counts and reports the day's sales to a computerized bookkeeping system by pressing one button.

However, a slower business, or one with just a few large monthly transactions, such as a small website design shop, dog-sitting service, or swimming pool repair company, would likely be fine if it were posted weekly or even monthly.

Use accounting software where possible. All but the smallest new businesses are well advised to use a package of accounting software to help keep their books. Micro-enterprises can use personal finance software like Quicken to get by.

Step 3: Creating Basic Financial Reports

Financial Reports are important because they bring together several key pieces of your business financial information. Think about it this way: while your income ledger may tell you that your business brought in a lot of money over the year, you won't know if you turned a profit against your total expenses without measuring your income. And even comparing your monthly income and expenses totals won't tell you if your credit customers are paying fast enough to keep an adequate cash flow through your business to pay your bills on time.

That's why financial reports are needed: to combine your ledger's data and form it into a shape that gives you the big picture of your business. The key reports you need to regularly create are a cash flow analysis, a forecast for profit and loss, and a balance sheet.

3.2 Why Is It Important To Keep Books?

Not only does proper bookkeeping ensure you meet your tax liability, but it can also provide a clearer picture of the financial well-being of your business, and even help you earn and save more money. That's because good bookkeeping will help you avoid potential penalties, fees, and unnecessary costs, find opportunities to save money, and help you make better business decisions.

Indeed, having accurate and up-to-date financial information available to you 365 days of the year can provide a range of far-reaching advantages for small business owners. Here are just a few: It can minimize an audit's probability and burden. Keeping reliable and up-to-date financial records will reduce the likelihood of being audited, but it can also keep an audit's hassle to a minimum in case one is conducted. After all, when the records are already well maintained and up to date, there's little reason to fear an audit. But without accurate records, it is hard to stay on top of the money flow in and out of business. Proper bookkeeping not only allows you to get a more accurate picture of the financial health of your business, but it can also help you anticipate and avoid any potential cash flow problems on the horizon.

It Will Improve Your Ability to Receive Funding

Books that are well maintained make it easier for small business owners to receive external financing, as they are often the first and most important records that loan providers and investors require. Even if at this time, you are not looking for outside financing, proper bookkeeping can accelerate the process in case of a crisis. After all, you probably don't want to spend a significant amount of time working on updating your books before you can solve it when faced with a critical cash-flow problem. Instead, proper bookkeeping can give you the assurance that your business is ready to pursue financing outside without any delay.

It Can Improve Your Invoicing Cycles.

You never have to worry about missing a payment to a vendor or not being compensated for your work when the invoicing is running smoothly.

Keeping track of payments will also enable you to gain a better understanding of how the business spends its money, which can help you solve redundancies and other ways to cut costs. It can also make sure you don't miss any payments that could otherwise lead to unnecessary late fees and penalties. And as disruptive as missing a payment to a vendor could be, letting your own invoices slip through the cracks is far more expensive. Proper bookkeeping ensures that at the right time, you send invoices to the right customers, as well as helping you manage and track your own receivable accounts to ensure that your work is always compensated.

It Will Reduce Your Payment Cycles

Every day you wait for a customer to receive an invoice is a day you will probably have to go without receiving payment. However, even if you can afford to wait for a few days for some payments, too many delays can add up to a real cash flow crisis. Ensuring you are properly compensated in a timely manner is one of the best things you can do to prevent a cash flow crunch from threatening a successful.

Without precise books, you run the risk of late paying employees, or the wrong amount, which can cause a whole range of headaches to both parties. For example, any misalignment between the stated income of the employee and its actual earnings could affect their tax filings. That doesn't even take into account a conversation's awkwardness over why you paid them inaccurately or way too late.

It Will Help You See the Forest through the Trees

If you update your books only a couple of times a year, you may miss crucial insights that can help you become a better business leader.

You are often forced to be reactive without accurate bookkeeping, as you will only become aware of issues when they become too obvious to miss.

Disorganized books not only make it harder to identify financial problems but also harder to solve. With accurate and up-to-date financial records, however, before they become critical, you will be able to identify and prevent potential threats to your business.

It's Never Been Easier

There was a time when small business owners had to do their own books, hire a full-time staffer or outsource their bookkeeping to a costly accounting firm, but now there is a fourth option that offers more flexibility, convenience, and cost-efficiency than all those that came before it.

3.3 Difference Between Book-Keeping and Accounting

When you start a small business first, you will hear the terms used almost interchangeably for bookkeeping and accounting. There is a difference in your business firm's bookkeeping and accounting. Bookkeeping is the practice of documenting your business transactions in your general ledger, the book, or software program, which has enclosed all the transactions of your business since its beginning. Accounting is the practice of analyzing your ledgers ' information and developing insights into your business ' financial decisions.

Bookkeeping

Bookkeeping is the process of keeping a daily record of all financial transactions in a company. The bookkeepers record the company's sales, expenses, cash, and bank transactions in a general ledger. The recording of transactions in your general ledger is one of the important habits you should develop when starting a business. Recording of such transactions is called publishing. In addition, a bookkeeper may generate invoices and/or full payroll.

All but the smallest businesses should set up and track the following nine accounts to provide adequate financial information for the accountant of the company's financial statements and taxes:

1. **Cash:** There are often two parts in the cash ledger, which are cash receipts and cash payments, which are also used to complete the cash budget.
2. **Receivable Accounts:** If your company allows credit accounts, then it has receivable accounts. This information is used for creating invoices and sending bills to your credit clients.
3. **Inventory:** If you're selling products instead of services, you've got inventory to track.
4. **Accounts Payable:** You will have accounts payable if you purchase items such as office supplies for your business, and you use credit. This budget is also called trade credit, and this is what the vendors owe. There is a trade credit cost associated with that.
5. **Loans Payable:** You must be able to track your due dates and payments if you have borrowed money to make bigger purchases.
6. **Sales:** You have to be able to track your sales, whether it's credit or money.
7. **Payroll Expenditures:** The cost of paying your staff.
8. **Purchases:** This includes raw material or finished goods. It is used in the cash budget and in the calculation on the income statement of the firm's Cost of goods sold.
9. **Owner's Draw:** This is the sum the owner of a small business takes from the firm.

Bookkeeping Methods

The two bookkeeping methods are single-and double-entry. Many businesses use the double-entry bookkeeping scheme, in which each account entry includes a similar and opposite entry to another account.

For example, a $10 cash sale would require posting two entries: a $10 debit entry to a "Cash" account, and a $10 credit entry to a "Revenue" account. A good bookkeeper's key attributes are being a stickler for accuracy and completeness. Since even the most thorough bookkeeper can make mistakes, a bookkeeper usually works under an accountant's direction, unless the business is very small. Some studies have found it might be best to have an external accountant. If the business is very small, it can be a lot like keeping your checkbook.

Accounting

Accounting was called Business Language. It is the process where financial information is measured, processed, and communicated. Accounting provides the business owner with knowledge about the tools, the finances, and the outcomes obtained by the business through its use. The accounting role is to maintain a record of the financial affairs of the enterprise. Accounting involves interpreting the numbers the bookkeeper has prepared to determine the financial health of the business. It also includes presenting a company's financial health, which involves preparing financial statements, as well as indicators that can be derived from them. In addition, the accounting function is to prepare the tax and other financial materials that are required.

Accounting Methods

There are two different accounting methods. One is based on the cash you got, and the cash you got. The other is spending on an accrual basis. If you have an inventory or a possibility of being audited, you are required to use accrual accounting under the General Accepted Accounting Principles (GAAP) established by the FASB.

Cash-based accounting is far simpler than accounting on an accrual basis.

You report revenue as you earn it in cash-based accounting, and record payments when they are made. This method is usually limited to small enterprises that do not have an inventory in the service industry.

The accrual accounting method is based on earning rather than receiving revenues. This could be thought of as transferring value between accounts. If you buy a point of sale terminal, you transfer the value to your equipment account from your cash account.

Credit is recorded on the cash account, and debit is recorded on account of the facilities. An account chart can help you decide when to make credit or debit accounts. They can also outsource the accounting function to a private entity. Both the bookkeeping and accounting functions are outsourced at some small businesses. If you outsource your accounting and bookkeeping, you will still want to be familiar with both of them in order to understand the reports you'll receive.

Chapter 04: Managing Profitability and Cash

Even though the business of doing business is driven by people, money fuels the engine. That money can be counted, compiled and presented in a number of different ways-ways that, in the right hands, can provide a steady flow of financial information to accomplish a number of key business functions, such as: maintaining information on bookkeeping: this includes keeping records of physical inventories, money due from others (accounts receivable), and money.

- **Paying taxes:** Federal, state, and local governments not only require the company to pay taxes but also keep records to support those payments.
- **Keeping score:** To know if you are going to be able to meet the expenses of next month or if the profitability and cash of your business are trending in the right direction, you need to keep track of the results of doing business.
- **Providing an information management tool:** Information fuels the decision-making process, and the more information you have as a small business owner, the better your choices can be. This chapter is about collecting financial information and using it.

A thorough review of this chapter, some time spent with your tax advisor, and several months reviewing your own statements, and you'll find out how to properly use your accounting system's financial information. Specifically, we focus on the information you can use to manage your cash flow, boost your profitability, and improve your chances of staying in the long haul business.

4.1 Success or Failure, It Depends On Cash-flow

Cash flow is the type of money that flows within a month from and into your company. Though it sometimes seems that cash flow just goes one direction-out of business-both directions run.

> ➢ Cash comes from customers or customers who buy your goods or services. If customers don't pay at purchase time, some of your cash flow comes from receivable account collections.
> ➢ Cash leaves your business in the form of expense payments, such as rent or mortgage, regular loan payments, and tax payments, and other accounts due.

Cash vs. Real Cash

Money is really cash-currency and paper money for some businesses, including restaurants, and some retailers. The business takes cash from clients and sometimes pays out in cash for its bills, particularly as they may not track revenue unless there are invoices or other paperwork.

Why is Cash Flow So Relevant?

Lack of cash is one of the most significant reasons why small businesses struggle.

The Small Business Administration says "insufficient cash reserves" are a major reason why startups don't succeed. It's called "running out of money," and shutting you down more quickly than anything else.

• **Starting a business:** The most difficult way to deal with cash flow issues when you start a business. You have a lot of expenses, and the money goes out quickly. And you may have no sales or paying customers. To get you started and going to a positive cash flow scenario, you will need some other immediate sources of cash, like a temporary line of credit.

- **Seasonal Business:** cash flow is especially important for seasonal businesses-those with large business fluctuations at different times of the year, such as holiday and summer businesses. It is tricky to manage cash flow in this type of business, but it can be achieved with caution.

- **Vs. Profit:** You can make a profit for your company but don't have any cash. How could this be? Cash businesses have a particular issue in keeping a record of the cash flow; the short answer is that profit is an accounting concept, while cash, as noted above, is just the amount in the account for the checking business. You can have properties, like receivable accounts (customers owing you money), but if you can't collect on what's owed, you won't have cash.

For a fact, the accounting system will indicate a disparity between cash and earnings. If your business is running on accrual accounting, you recognize revenue when the invoice is sent, even if the customer has not paid. You may be showing a profit in this case but don't have the cash.

How to Analyze Cash Flow?

The best way to keep track of the cash flow is to run a cash flow report in your business. For example:

- What happens if a client pays a bill in cash?
- What happens to cash when your business buys deliveries?
- What happens when you buy a computer in cash?
- What happens when you pay an employee or an independent contractor in cash?

You may need to keep track of the cash flow at times on a weekly, perhaps even a daily basis. To grab this tip deeper:

a. Look at your total sales as of the end of this month.

b. Add up the purchases you made, which still have to be paid for.

c. The difference is what you'll need to put in to live even as wages.

How Do Business Owners of Cash Flow Problems Force Bad Decisions?

If you get anything from this site, know that there are three reasons why businesses fail: it's due to cash flow, cash flow, and yes, cash flow. First, to make one thing clear, profits do not equal cash flow. The situation where profit and cash flow are at odds is very common for a small business that has to invest in assets to grow. The reasons are always visible on the balance sheet.

Cash flow measures the company's ability to pay out its bills. The cash balance is the received cash, minus the cash paid out during the period. This is where cash flow management can get things tricky. Under the U.S. Bank study, poor cash management accounts for 82 percent of business failures. Small business owners and CEOs need to make decisions with the cash flow of their business that can sometimes cause negative long term results. Business decisions, in some cases, lead to cash-flow problems. Once you're in the cash flow crunch, lack of resources and fear further impact your decision-making ability. This can lead to bad decisions in three main areas of your business:

Pricing: Lowering your job prices or offering discounts/promotion to get any job, which can result in lower margins than your target margins, causing cash flow problems. Problems with cash flow cause you not to look at your pricing model or experiment with value pricing because you are too afraid to lose business.

Hiring / Firing: You are hanging on to hiring because cash is tight, but you have the work coming in and because of the lack of proper resources that affects consistency, scheduling, and customer service.

Which then provokes negative reviews and unsatisfied clients. You hesitate to fire because the search, replacement, re-training, etc. costs are greater than fighting with a mediocre employee. You keep bad customers because you need the cash flow, but bad customers either don't pay timely, cause pain in the service team, or don't meet your target profit margins.

Spending: You're not spending in places where you should be spending because you feel you can't afford it. For instance, you may not be doing a marketing campaign with your business marketing, because you don't want to spend the money and are too worried about the ROI. You don't hire in Sales, because you don't want to spend the money paying someone else. Because of the costs that may be involved, you don't take advantage of opportunities or take informed risks to support your business.

4.2 Making Sense of Financial Statements

The accounting system you are using, whether manual or computer-driven, will eventually produce two financial statements: the profit and loss statement (also known as the income statement) and the balance sheet. Both of these statements are produced at the end of the accounting period of a business, usually monthly, quarterly, or annually.

They recommend that you read (or prepare) the financial statements as frequently as possible, the most important being usually the monthly statements. If you are able to generate your financial statements internally through your accounting system, we recommend you generate your statements monthly. If for some reason, monthly statements are unlikely, quarterly statements will do so, but do not fall into the trap other small businesses do by producing their statements only once or twice a year.

1. Profit And Loss Account

Even if you don't need money from a bank or other lender for your small business project, you'll need several financial statements to help you make some decisions. The most important financial statement of any business requirement is a statement of profit and loss (called a "P&L"). Sometimes, it is called a statement of income.

The statement shows the business's sales and expenditures, and subsequent profit or loss, over a specific period of time (a month, quarter, or year).

When Do You Need to Prepare a Statement About Profit and Loss?

- **Periodic P&L:** Every business needs to periodically prepare and revise its statement of profit and loss-at at least every quarter. Reviewing the statement of profit and loss helps businesses make decisions and prepare the tax return. Your business tax return will use the P&L information as the basis for calculating net income to determine the income tax that your business is required to pay.
- **Pro Forma P&L:** A new business has to generate a statement of profit and loss at startup. This statement is pro forma created, meaning it's projected into the future.

What details do I need to prepare for this statement?

Most of the information for this statement comes from your monthly budget for the first year (cash flow statement), and from your tax advisor's estimated depreciation calculations. In particular, you'll need to:

1. A transaction listing of all your business checking account transactions and all purchases made using your business credit cards.
2. Include any small cash transactions or other cash transactions that you get receipts for.

3. For revenue, you will need to list all sources of income- checks, payments by credit card, etc. These should be found on your bank statement.
4. You will also need information regarding any sales reductions, such as discounts or returns.

If you are using business accounting software, you should include the profit and loss statement in the regular reports. Even if you have this report in your system, you still should be aware of what information is required to prepare the report.

Adding Cash Transactions to Your P&L

Don't forget to add cash transactions, revenue, as well as expenses. Even if you have business accounting software, cash transactions may still need to be recorded manually, like cash for small cash and revenues. Use a cash transaction form (available from the office supply companies) or a quick invoice when you accept cash from customers. Save the file for cash payments. These receipts are particularly important for expenses relating to business driving and business meals.

Preparing a Pro Forma (Projected Profit and Loss Statement)

If you start a business, you don't have the information to prepare a true P&L statement yet, so you have to guess. A pro forma statement is generally prepared for each month of the first business year, but your lender may require you to add more months or years to the projection to show the break-even point when your business is consistently generating positive cash flow.

a. List all possible expenses and overestimate them so you won't be surprised. Don't forget to add the "miscellaneous" category and an amount.
b. Estimate sales by month. Sales under-estimate, both in terms of timing and amount.

c. For some period of time, the gap between expenses and revenue is usually negative. You will calculate the negative sums to give you an idea of how much you will need to borrow to get your business started.

Preparing a Periodic Declaration of Profit and Loss

The process of preparation and information required is the same whether you are preparing a statement at start-up or using it for tax preparation or business analysis. You'll have a quarterly amount for each row, and then a year total.

a. First, show your net income from business (usually called "Sales") for each quarter of the year. If you wish, you can break down the income into sub-sections to show income from different sources.
b. Then spell out your business expenses for every quarter. Show each expense as Sales percentage. All expenses are expected to total 100 percent of sales.
c. Then, show the difference as earnings between Sales and Expenses. Sometimes this is called EBITDA (earnings before interest, taxes, amortization, and depreciation).
d. Then show total interest for the year on your business debt and subtract from EBITDA.
e. Next list Net income taxes (usually estimated) and subtract.
f. Lastly, show total yearly depreciation and amortization, and subtract.

The number you now have is net earnings, or profit-or loss-from your business.

2. Balance Sheet of a Small Business

It knows what counts for a balance sheet. At the end of the item, you can find our sample balance sheet. It is a type of a business's condition at a given time, usually at the close of an accounting period.

A balance sheet includes capital assets, liabilities, and equity of owners or stockholders. Assets and liabilities are divided into short and long-term liabilities, including cash accounts such as checking, money market, or securities of government.

Assets must have equal liabilities, plus equity of owners, at any given time. An asset is anything the business owns, which has monetary value. Liabilities are the creditors ' claims against the firm's assets. So when you're creating a balance sheet, you have to make sure it balances. The way you do this is to increase or decrease the sheet side of the liabilities so that it is equal to the side of the assets. More specifically, the part you adjust from the side of the liabilities is the equity of the owners.

It may sound like owners ' equity falls under the liabilities category, but essentially you can think of it as the value owed to the owners from the business. In other words, the assets on the left side of the balance sheet are carefully added, and then all the liabilities on the right side of the balance sheet are added, and the liabilities subtracted from the assets. The net number is the equity of the owners. Of course, if the liabilities are greater than the assets, it is possible that the owners ' equity is negative.

What is used for a Balance Sheet?

Unable to account without a balance sheet. Are businesses in a position to expand? Can the business handle the normal financial ebbs and revenue and expense flows with ease? Or should the company take immediate action to bolster cash reserves?

Balance sheets are able to identify and analyze trends, especially in the receivables and payables sector.

Is the cycle of admissions lengthening? Can we more aggressively collect receivables? Was indebtedness uncollectable? Has the company slowed down payables in order to prevent an imminent shortage of cash?

Similarly, if you are a sole proprietorship, your personal balance sheet is what matters, because the business does not exist as a separate legal entity.

How do I format a Sheet Balance?

Assets

Assets are subdivided into current and long term assets to reflect the ease with which each asset can be liquidated. Cash is considered the liquid of all assets, for obvious reasons.

1. Current assets

Current assets are any assets that, within one calendar year, can be easily converted into cash. Definitions of current assets include checking or cash market accounts, receivable accounts, and receivable notes that are due within one year.

- **Cash:** The most liquid of all short-term assets is the money available immediately, such as in the checking accounts.
- **Receivable accounts:** This is money owed to the company for purchases made by customers, suppliers, and other vendors.
- **Notes receivable:** Current assets are receivable notices due within one year. Long-term assets should be considered as notes which cannot be collected within one year.

Long-term assets include land, buildings, machinery, and commercially used vehicles.

- **Land:** It is considered a fixed asset, but, unlike other fixed assets, it is not depreciated because the land is considered an asset that never wears out.
- **Buildings:** Constructions are classified as fixed assets and are depreciated over time.

- **Office equipment:** It includes copiers, fax machines, printers, and laptops that your business uses.
- **Machinery:** This figure represents the machinery and equipment used to manufacture your product in your warehouse. Machinery examples could include lathes, conveyor belts, or a printing press.
- **Vehicles:** All vehicles used in your business are included here.
- **Total fixed assets:** This is the total dollar value of all of your business ' fixed assets, less any accumulated depreciation.

Liabilities and Shareholders ' Equity

It covers all loans and liabilities that the company owes to foreign investors, suppliers, or banks that are due within one year, plus owners ' equities. That side of the balance sheet is often referred to simply as "liabilities."

1. Current liabilities

This is the sum of all current liabilities owed to creditors to be paid within one year.

- **Accounts payable:** This includes all short-term obligations to creditors, suppliers, and other vendors that your business owes. Accounts payable may include deliveries and credit-acquired materials.
- **Notes payable:** This is money owed on a one year or less short term collection cycle. This may include banknotes, mortgage commitments, or fees for cars.
- **Payroll accrued and withholding:** This includes any earned salaries or withholdings due to or for employees but not yet paid.

2. Long-Term Liabilities

These are any debts or obligations owed by the business that are due from the current date of more than one year.

- **Mortgage note payable:** This is the mortgage balance that extends beyond the current year. For example, you may have paid off a fifteen-year mortgage note for three years, of which the remaining eleven years (excluding the current year) are considered to be long term.

3. **Owners ' Equity**

This is sometimes referred to as equity of the stockholders. The equity of the owners consists of the initial investment in the business as well as any retained earnings, which are reinvested in the business. Remember, total liabilities must be equal to the assets, including owners ' equities. The way you achieve balance is by summing up all of the business ' assets and then subtracting all the liabilities except for owners ' equity. The remaining amount is equity to the owners.

4. **Common Stock**

This is stock sold as part of the company's initial or later-stage investment. That stock remains fixed on the company's books at its initial valuation.

5. **Retained Earnings**

These are earnings that are reinvested in the business once any distributions to shareholders have been deducted, such as dividend payments. Retained earnings are measured through the subtraction of common stock from the equity of shareholders.

6. **Total Liabilities And Equity of Owners**

This includes all debts and monies owed to external creditors, vendors, or banks and the remaining monies owed to shareholders, including retained earnings reinvested in the business.

4.3 Managing Your Inventory

Managing a small business inventory helps you track and control your supply, so you can optimize your inventory and manage your stock without spending more time or money than you need. While inventory control software may at first seem intimidating, you can get into it relatively easily, particularly if you start early.

What is inventory management, and why small business is critical of it?

Inventory management is inventory science, where you use the information from your inventory sheet to create usable data, but you don't need a data analytics mastery to make it work, just a bit of practice. In fact, most maths are automated with a dedicated inventory management system. Inventory management helps you keep track of sales, shipments, and manufacturing, so you can see which products are being sold, where, and how much. (It's science, not magic, we promise!) It lets you predict your entire supply and demand curve, adjust shipments and deliveries, or even manufacture precisely to suit your needs. All of this allows you to reduce the cost of inventories to increase productivity. It also lets you reduce over-and under-stock costs and headaches.

- **Customer Service**

Customer Service Inventory Management is crucial because it enables you to avoid faux pas, such as allowing customers to order products that are no longer in stock. You will also be able to track production and backorders using a good inventory management system, so you can tell interested customers when the item will be on stock. Backorders, or orders placed when a product is not available for shipment, are also useful for tracking demand so you can improve the availability of high-demand items.

- **Theft Control**

While not always a problem for small businesses, particularly those primarily on the web, theft control is important when you start taking on staff or have a physical shop. Inventory management allows you to see how many products you have at any given time, with the associated sales revenue, so it is easy to see when something is missing. Hopefully, this never happens, but it's something you should remember.

- **Supply and Demand**

Long-term supply and demand data can tell you which products you are selling, which customers want more, and which you should stop.

- **Inventory Tracking**

Market Tracking helps you to monitor your inventory on the basis of high-sales products and things that are not available. In this way, you can market the items that are most likely to sell, rather than advertising to those that don't. While that might sound a bit doomy and gloomy, every business lifecycle has a point where inventory management becomes a necessity.

Inventory Management Techniques

That is said, inventory management is only as powerful as the way you use it.

To have the inventory management set up by the experts who made the software is well worth the extra time and money. Work with them to ensure that you use the right techniques and features to get the most bang for your buck. Let's look at some of the inventory-control techniques that you might choose to use in your own warehouse.

- **Quantity Economic Order**

Economic order quantity, or EOQ, is a formula for the ideal order quantity that a company needs to buy for its inventory, with a set of variables such as total production costs, demand rate, and other factors. EOQ's overall aim is to minimize associated costs. The formula is used to identify the largest number of units of product to minimize purchases. For most companies, this helps to free up tied cash in inventory.

- **Minimum Quantity to Order**

Minimum order quantity (MOQ) on the supplier side is the smallest amount of set stock that a supplier is willing to sell. If retailers cannot afford to buy a product's MOQ, the supplier will not sell it to you. For example, inventory items that cost more to produce typically have a smaller MOQ than cheaper items that are easier to make and are more cost-effective.

- **Analysis of ABC**

This inventory categorization technique divides subjects into three categories to identify items that impact heavily on the overall cost of inventory.

   a. Category A is your most valuable product, which contributes the most to your overall profit.
   b. Category B is the most and the least valuable product which falls somewhere between.
   c. Category C is for small transactions that are vital to the overall profit but which do not matter to the company individually.

- **Managing Inventories Just-in-Time**

Just-in-time (JIT) inventory management is a technique that arranges suppliers ' commands of raw materials in direct relation to production schedules.

Instead of ordering too much and risking deadstock, companies receive inventory on an as-needed basis. Deadstock is an inventory that customers have never sold or used before being deleted from sales status.

- **Inventory of the Safety Stocks**

Managing inventory of security stocks is ordering extra inventory beyond expected demand. This technique is used to prevent stock outs that are typically caused by incorrect forecasting or unforeseen customer demand changes.

- **FIFO, like LIFO**

LIFO and FIFO are mechanisms by which inventory costs are calculated. FIFO, or First in, First out, assume the first to sell the older inventory. FIFO's a great way to keep a fresh inventory. LIFO, or Last-in, First-out, assumes that the newer inventory is usually first sold. LIFO helps prevent bad inventories from happening.

How Product Management can be used to Boost Sales and ROI?

Product management, when used correctly, will boost the revenues and ROI (return on investment). You can boost revenue on products by streamlining your production, shipping, and sales process to ensure that you meet demand without going over, and by saving as much money as possible one very part of delivery.

- **Inventory Analysis**

It's pretty easy to analyze the inventory, and you can do that with Excel. The simplest method is to organize products in order to get the most sales, allowing you to focus your attention on those products so that you can meet the demand for the product.

- **Shrinkage Inventory**

One of the easiest ways for small businesses to save money with inventory management is by reducing inventory. You can then reduce the amount of excess inventory that you have on hand, and supply the number of products that are most likely to sell to your consignment shops, shops, or web store warehouse. Important considerations include making adjustments to suit different seasons and sales periods (such as holidays) to meet the demand for that season appropriately. Considering social or world events that could make your product sell faster over a given period of time (I.E., the Super Bowl, if you sell products related to football) are also crucial to the success of inventory shrinking.

The idea of inventory shrinkage is that you can reduce the cost of buying inventory, reduce storage, and therefore save money by just bringing in enough inventory to meet the demand. It can be backfired if you have not supplied at the proper time, but this shouldn't happen with a good analytics system. If you pay a lot for deliveries, though, that might not be the best way to go.

Tips for Managing Inventory of Small Business

Here you'll find the ten critical tips for managing your inventory efficiently to increase profitability and maximize cash flow.

- **Put Your Inventory First**

Classifying your inventory into priority groups can help you understand which ones you need to order more and more frequently, and which are important to your business but can be expensive and move slower.

Typically experts suggest separating your inventory into groups A, B, and C. Items in group and are items with higher tickets you need fewer of.

Goods in group C are goods of a lower cost whose inventory quickly turns over. The B group is what remains–those items that are priced moderately and move out of the door more slowly than items C but faster than items A.

- **Has your Inventory Audited?**

Some companies do an exhaustive count once a year. Others do spot checks of their hottest items monthly, weekly, or even daily. Many do the above. Whatever you do, make it a point to regularly physically count your inventory to ensure it matches what you think you've got.

- **Analyze the Performance of Suppliers**

An unreliable supplier can put your inventory in trouble. If you have a supplier who is regularly late with delivery or often shorts an order, then it is time to take action. Discuss the issues with your manufacturer to find out what the problem is. Be prepared to switch partners, or contend with unpredictable stock levels and the resulting potential to run out of inventory.

- **Practice the Inventory Rule of 80/20**

As a general rule, 80% of your earnings come from 20% of your stock. Make inventory management a priority for those items. Comprehend the sales lifecycle of these items completely, including how many you sell in a week or a month, and monitor them closely.

- **Be Consistent About How You are Getting Stuck**

Making sure incoming inventory is processed may seem like common sense, but do you have a standard process that everyone goes through? Or does it different for every employee who receives and processes incoming stock? Small discrepancies in how new stocks are taken in might have you scratching your head at the end of the month or year, wondering why your numbers are not aligned with your POs. Make sure all staff receiving stock do so the same way, that all boxes received and unpacked together are verified, accurately counted, and accurately checked.

- **Sales track**

Again, that seems like a no-brainer, but at the end of the day, it goes beyond simply adding up sales. On a daily basis, you should understand what items were sold and how many, and update the total inventories. But more than that, this data will need to be analyzed. Do you know when certain items sell or drop off faster? Are they seasonal? Is there a particular weekday when you are selling certain items? Do certain items sell together almost always? Knowing not only the total sales but the broader picture of how things look is important to keep the inventory in check.

- **Order Yourself Out Restocks**

Some vendors offer you to do inventory and reordering. But remember that your salespeople don't have the same priorities that you do. They seek to move their items while you seek to store items that are most profitable for your business. Take the time to check yourself on inventory and order restocks of all your items.

- **Invest in Technology to Manage Inventories**

If you are a small enough business, it's doable to handle the first eight items on this list manually, with spreadsheets and notebooks. Good software for inventory management makes all of those tasks easier. Before choosing a software solution, make sure you understand what you need, provide you with important analytics for your business, and make it easy to use.

- **Using Technology is Well Incorporated**

Inventory software is not the only technology that can help you manage your stock. Things such as mobile scanners and POS systems can help keep you on track. Prioritize systems that work together when investing in technology.

4.4 Setting up Payrolls

It seems easy to set up payroll for small businesses, but there are a number of steps involved that need to be mindful of through small businesses. Failure to take one of those steps can result in costly fines and sanctions. That is why we created this easy-to-follow, nine-step guide on how to set up your small business payroll. You should check with your accounting professional as you learn how to set up payroll to make sure you meet all the requirements for your particular situation. An attorney with experience of your state's labor laws is also a valuable resource during the process of establishing a payroll system.

Nevertheless, our payroll setup guide will help you tackle this exciting yet challenging process with greater confidence, which will eventually allow you to recruit the help you need. As a reminder, setting up your small business payroll is an intricate and precise process.

These nine steps on how to set up payroll will serve as an outline of the process, but each small business will have its own requirements and logistics to address as it first establishes payroll. Here's how to set up payroll in nine steps for your small business:

Step 1: Review of the US. Labor Department Website

There are certain rules that apply to most businesses in the U.S. These rules include the legislation on minimum wage, the Family and Medical Leave Act, and the rules on overtime, just to name a few. Start setting up your Small Business Payroll by reviewing the US Topics section. Labor Department website. Navigate to the DOL website's First Step Poster Advisor section to decide which posters you need to view in order to comply with federal employment regulations.

Step 2: Review your State's Labor Website Department

In the U.S. The labor department regulates federal employment law, and each state has its own labor regulations. As you set up payroll for your small business, you must be mindful of both federal and state legislation. What if the website of your state's labor department provides contradictory information to what you see in the US? Labor department website? Generally speaking, the law favors the employee, and so you should abide by the rules that benefit the employee most. Federal law, for example, dictates that overtime should be paid once an employee exceeds 40 hours in a workweek. However, some states that mandate overtime based on the number of hours worked in a day.

If in doubt, check for your state with your accountant or a labor lawyer who is versed in the law. Not only will this keep you out of legal trouble, but it will also help ensure that your employees are treated fairly, which in turn will lead to a happier workforce.

Step 3: Fix your Payroll Schedule

Many businesses operate payroll weekly, bi-weekly, or half-monthly. Determine the schedule for your payroll you wish to use. Keep in mind the cash flow for your business as you determine how often you would like to pay your employees. There are strict laws on paying employees on time, and while you may be able to change your payroll schedule, you should not do so too often. Keep in mind the laws for your state may dictate the minimum frequency of your payroll schedule, so make sure that you check your payroll schedule against the requirements on the labor website of your state department.

Step 4: Write a Handbook for your Employees

Now that you know which laws in your state relating to payroll, it's time to write your employee manual. If you cringe with the thought of writing anything, don't worry. A number of online resources can help you craft your employee handbook, or you can hire a professional human resources services to write one for you.

When registered, you can ask the state to send your employee handbook to an attorney who is trained in employment law. They will make sure that your handbook contains no language that establishes a contractual relationship between you and your employees. It will also ensure that you have understood the laws in your state regarding payroll and employment issues correctly.

Step 5: Use your Federal Employer Identification Number (FEIN or EIN) for application

For tax filing purposes, many sole proprietors use their Social Security Number. You must, however, use a Federal Employer Identification Number, or FEIN or EIN, for employment purposes.

When issued, the EIN is the number on all business tax filings and forms that you will be using.

That is why many accounting professionals are strongly encouraging business owners to get an EIN as soon as they start their business. It's easy to obtain a FEIN if you don't already have one.

Step 6: Apply for the Accounts of your State withholding and Unemployment Insurance

You may be required to withhold state income taxes and pay into the unemployment insurance fund of your state, depending on your state. Certain states also have local tax withholding requirements. On the websites for your state's tax commission and unemployment security commission, you can often find information regarding your employment situation. These websites are, however, sometimes confusing and difficult to navigate. As was the case with Step 2, check with your accountant or jobs lawyer about the laws pertaining to your state.

Once you determine which tax accounts you need, it is time for those accounts to apply. Most states allow you to apply online for these accounts, although some still require that you fax or mail in your application. Allow your State to set up your tax accounts and provide you with the numbers for up to four weeks.

Step 7: Include in your Calendar the Payroll Schedule and the Due Dates for Tax Filings

Now that you have set your payroll schedule and are applying for your FEIN, state withholding, and unemployment insurance accounts, you need to make sure that you adhere to all the relevant deadlines. Start by entering dates on your calendar for payroll.

Then enter your due dates for filing the payroll tax. Keep in mind that you may have different due dates to send taxes and return information.

State deadlines could be different from federal due dates, too. Review all the information you received along with the number of your state withholding and unemployment insurance account, and the Publication 15 you downloaded in Step 4.

Step 8: Decide Who Will Get Your Payroll Administered

Will you handle payroll in-house or use a payroll service provider? Both choices have both advantages and inconveniences. In-house payroll handling gives you a little more flexibility when it comes to processing the payroll. Payroll service providers often require three-to five-day lead times and charge a rush fee if you do not submit payroll information within their deadlines. Payroll service providers, however, often assume all responsibility for the timely filing of tax payments and returns, and this is attractive to the busy small business owner.

It is strongly recommended using an online payroll platform such as Intuit Online Payroll or Gusto if you choose to handle payroll in-house. This will streamline the administration of your payroll and help ensure that taxes are paid, and returns are filed on time. You may wonder at this point why you were going through Steps 1-6. A payroll service provider will, in many cases, apply to you for your tax account numbers. Most payroll software programs remind you when the time is right to run payroll, make tax payments, and file returns of information. So why did you go through those six first steps if you could automate them?

In our experience, small business payroll is most often incorrectly set up when the business owner has no involvement in the process. Working closely with a payroll service provider or using payroll software will streamline the ongoing payroll process, but knowing the standards and laws as they pertain to your employees is still crucial.

For your small business, setting up the payroll for your first employees is a big step. This milestone means the business is one step closer to its autonomous operation. Employees allow small business owners to do the things that really build the business, rather than focus on doing all of the work themselves. And the payroll system for a small business should do the same — take busy work off the hands of a small business owner so they can continue strategizing and growing their business. Don't let the prospect of putting up your growing team's payroll make you hesitate to hire the help you need. Now that you've been through this thorough process of setting up the payroll, you can focus on training your new employee. Your first payroll run will be smooth, and the payroll will fit into your operations seamlessly.

4.5 Managing your Account Receivables and Creditors

Many business people aren't economists. They're just ingenious or ambitious people who have creative business ideas and want to put them into organized practice.

We may, however, lack knowledge of certain professional financial terminology. If they want to communicate on an equal footing with their customers and business associates, they need to master those sentences. Business owners need to be versed in financial concepts. We have therefore provided a thorough analysis of two major cash principles that every single business owner needs to learn-receivable accounts and payable accounts. While learning the ABCs of cash flow through these two activities, you will also have the opportunity to learn more about various strategies to keep the business in order with these two factors. They, too, are the crucial precondition for seamless business growth.

Receivable accounts= Assets to be Charged

Simply put; receivable accounts are all payments that other business entities are obliged to pay to your business for services or goods purchased. Let's say you are running a business in the field of building materials, for example. Various construction companies will be purchasing your products. Accounts receivable are the invoices you issue to those clients.

You have sold a few goods for which you expect payment. Because those payments make your balance sheet's revenue side, they are considered your assets. If your customers are honest and reliable business partners, they will pay on time for their obligations. The key element of every successful business is being paid on time. You don't need to have a weak spot for late payers, because of that. On the contrary, business owners should bring along a set of clear rules to deal with such customers.

Accounts payable= Accounts payable

In contrast to accounts payable, accounts payable include all debts payable by your business to other companies. Let's get back to the previous paragraph on the construction materials business. Running such a business means you are buying materials from other companies, too.

Accounts payable include each brick or plank you add to your stock. The moment your company receives an invoice from another organization, it becomes your liability. A potential problem arises here if you don't cover your debts on time. You can never tell nowadays when your business might need to take out a loan or make any other deal with your bank.

Not paying your debts according to the agreed due dates will affect your credit score for the business. That will treat your business as an unreliable entity.

This could disqualify you from reaching a financial deal with a bank or any other financial institution.

In fact, failure to pay your commitments within time limits will also place your own company at risk. So, it's clear that sorting out immediately payable accounts as they arrive is a must. But what can you do to meet your ends and to manage your obligations as quickly as possible?

Ask for Special Conditions Beforehand

If you are in a payer's position, you can try to negotiate some flexible terms for your business. Speak with your vendors in line with that, and ensure certain special conditions in advance. Be aware, however, that there is something you need to prepare to offer them in return. For example, if you wish to order a large number of items from the same vendor, it would be a smart move to ask them to pay them in multiple installments.

On the one hand, as those goods are being sold, you will pay them out. That would keep more cash in your pocket for the daily business errands. On the other hand, the vendor will benefit from that deal as well. They will get assets over a certain period of time, which will give them a constant cash inflow. Additionally, if you manage to put them on the market, it's highly likely that you will order the same products from them again.

If you anticipate you won't be able to pay them on time, it's also wise to contact your supplier. Since your payable accounts will depend on numerous factors, sometimes, you just don't manage to set up a budget that will cover all of your expenses.

If you experience such an inconvenience, don't even think about ignoring your salesperson. Instead of eluding your bill, please inform the vendor of your difficulties beforehand.

We also know what it looks like to be in the midst of a financial struggle. So the best thing you can do is to take an assertive attitude and address your supplier about your late payment.

Offer Unique Terms of Payment

The key goal of each business is to maintain steady cash flow, both at the receiving and expenditure ends. Following are the techniques into practice in your work:

- **Various Payment Methods for International Clients**

Working with global companies is a great opportunity for your business. Therefore let them choose how they are going to transfer their money to your account. The better they have, the more choices.

- **Reasonable Payment Deadlines**

These days, modern business deals are closed and executed in short periods of time, and money flows rapidly. Even if it's a longer project, they set milestones at that pace. Your profitability will be affected by long payment periods. So limit your customers to a payment period of three weeks. You might think about extending this deadline to your long-term or VIP customers, though.

- **Fast Payer Discounts**

Motivate the customers to make their payments as soon as possible by offering fast payer discounts. For example, make some early payer categories and decide how big discounts they will get for those payments.

- **Late Client Fees**

Inform your clients that if they miss the deadlines, you'll have to charge them extra fees.

Nonetheless, make sure that during the negotiations or even in the estimation (when working on a project), this note is explicitly mentioned somewhere. Finally, don't forget to include this note on your invoices, too. This reminder of three levels should be nudging them to pay you on time.

- **Note forwarding**

The most efficient way to reduce the number of late accounts receivable in advance is to remind your partners and customers of their due payments. This proactive approach will yield dual advantages. The other side will, for starters, have enough time to prepare assets and make the payment on time. You will also develop a closer relationship with your partners to enable them to settle their accounts payable on time.

- **Show Tolerance**

Set a grace period for your debtors to allow them to pay you with no official reminders sent. For example, you might accept a 5-day delay in payment. All that is beyond that, however, requires a course of determined actions. If the same customer repeatedly misses the deadline at regular intervals, contact them to check that their dates for invoices are correct.

- **Political Official Reminder**

A client who has ignored two preceding ultrasensitive features requires a harsher response. Consequently, send them an official reminder. You should not sound aggressive or impatient, either. Send them a polite template reminder of their corporate debts. Give them a new deadline (this will take seven days) and attach the invoice to that letter.

- **Serious Legal Warning**

Consumers who turn their ears deaf to all of your requests require a different way of communication. You should treat them the same way because they don't show understanding for your situation.

You will need to take legal action against them. Sending this kind of letter of request is the last step before starting a legal proceeding. Don't send this final warning, though, before you're absolutely sure you're ready to settle that case in court. All the notes that you send to your debtors will record the financial results. It will, in return, be an important piece of evidence in case you need to seek justice before legal institutions.

How to spot a payer in trouble?

There are numerous legal mechanisms to protect you and help you get what's yours back. Still, this process can become a long-lasting problem. Until you start working with a partner, you should spend more time in preparation and analysis to stop this tiresome process. Fortunately, we are living in a time when every single bit (and byte) of information is available by mouse click.

So you should carry out a thorough analysis of your potential business partners in advance. It could seem like a strenuous task at first. Even so, it will save you all the trouble that late or never-paying collaborations could cause. So, to minimize aggravation when dealing with your receivable accounts, cover the following points:

- **Social media and online checking:** Check their Facebook business page, LinkedIn profile, and other professional accounts when you contact a customer. That way, you'll gather more information about their lifestyles and habits. Also, check the status of their business. In the US, for example, you can visit the U.S. To learn more about company filings, the Securities and Exchange Commission website. Find out if it has a similar register in your country. It will help you get the gist of the business politics of your potential partner.

- **Feedback from consumers and suppliers:** You can get a lot of information from the feedback from others. Since freelancers are among the most endangered, payment-wise businesspeople, they should double-check every potential client. In line with that, professional websites can serve a great purpose, as you can get immediate insight into the portfolios and reviews on those channels for everyone.

- **Farewell repeat eluders:** The saying' Once bitten, twice shy' should be borne in mind when it comes to repeating financial obligations eluders. Most business owners don't like to abandon their clients, and some businessmen are likely to excuse irresponsible behavior and turn a new leaf over. However, if the same customer continues to show the same irrational attitude and does not fulfill your payment agreements, you should simply stop working with them and free time and space for more reliable customers.

The business market dictates numerous rules that must be met to make your business prosper. Because of that, you should stick to these values and tailor your professional effort to conditions outside. Inside your business, however, you will still have a wide range of features that require continuous work.

A positive ratio between accounts receivable and accounts payable is what keeps every business alive. Business people who manage to keep a regular inflow of earned assets and manage their obligations properly are more likely to achieve their business goals.

4.6 Understanding Key ratios and Percentages

Before you can take the numbers produced by the P & L and the balance sheet and turn them into practical management tools, you need to remember two overall points about the numbers, ratios, and percentages that come from those financial statements:

1. **Comparisons work best:** Numbers, ratios, and percentages are most useful compared to other numbers, ratios, and percentages, as explained earlier. Your company may have what appears to be a respectable percentage of net profit on its sales, but if that percentage is lower than it was the previous year during the same period, there may be danger ahead. Numbers are most effective when they can be used to identify trends-and it always takes a comparison of numbers over time to identify trends.
2. **The sector matters:** Acceptable figures may not be acceptable in one industry in another. The numbers they produce vary widely between industries. If you're in the software business, for example, you may be disappointed with an IS-percent profit return on your sales dollar (we'll explain what that means later in this chapter). Nonetheless, if you are in the grocery store market, you will probably be delighted with a return on sales in the S-percent range.

Key-terms:

If you don't know the acceptable ratios and percentages in your industry, contact your appropriate trade association. Most trade associations can give you the benchmark ratios and percentages that you need to know to compare your own business to industry averages. In the following sections, we explain the percentages and ratios most commonly used that should be considered by a small business owner.

1. **Return on Sales (R.O.S.)**

Return on Sales (R.O.S.) is a percentage of net pre-tax profits (from P & L) divided by total sales (also from P & L). The resulting figure measures the overall efficiency of your firm in converting a dollar of sales into a dollar of profit. To RO.S. This depends very much on what type of business you are doing. To the RO.S. Is a great figure you and your staff can focus on? Tracking, understanding, and explaining are relatively easy. Some businesses use this percentage as a business-wide scorecard to help their employees understand how businesses make money and, in turn, motivate them to do their part to ensure and improve profitability. (Most employees think they make a lot, a lot more money than they actually do.)

2. **Equity Return (R.O.E.)**

Equity Return (R.O.E.) is a percentage determined by dividing pre-tax profits (from P & L) by equity/net value (from the balance sheet). The resulting figure represents the return you made on the dollars you invested (your equity) in your company. Over several years, if your equity return is not higher than or about 5 percent (which is the average return on money invested in such secure investments as short-term, high-quality bonds), you may want to consider selling your business and investing the proceeds in bonds. Your return would be much the same, your risk a lot less, and the work.

3. **The Gross Margin**

Gross margin is a percentage determined by subtracting your cost of sold goods (from the P & L) from total sales (also from the P & L).

This figure represents the effective total markup of your business on products sold prior to deducting your operating expenses.

How good your gross margin depends on your business, your industry, and what you sell. It is here that the trend is particularly important. You want to see an improvement over a period of time, rather than a reduction in gross margin.

4. Quick Ratio

The quick ratio is a ratio determined by dividing current assets (from the balance sheet) by current (also in the balance sheet) liabilities. The resulting figure measures the liquidity of your business (the ability to raise immediate cash from the sale of your assets); so, this ratio is of great interest to your lenders in particular. The higher the rapid ratio, the more liquid your business will become. Rapid ratios greater than 2-to-1 are generally considered healthy; anything less is questionable. The trend here is particularly important once again. You want to see a rapid ratio growing over a period of time, rather than decreasing.

5. Debt-to-Equity Ratio

The debt-to-equity ratio is a ratio determined by dividing equity/net value (from the balance sheet) by debt/total debt (also from the balance sheet). The resulting ratio shows how much ownership of the business (represented by equity / net worth) and how much ownership of its creditors (represented by debt / total liabilities) is.

6. Inventory Turn

Inventory turn is the number of times in a year that your inventory turns over. You determine the number by dividing by your average inventory (starting + ending+ 2) the cost of the goods sold (from the P & L). If your starting stock (on Jan. 1) was $100,000, and your ending stock (on Dec. 31) was $150,000, your average stock would be $125,000.

The figure which results from the inventory turn calculation shows how well you are managing your inventory. The higher the number, the more times your stock has turned, which is always better. The number of times your inventory turns depends heavily on the industry (manufacturer, wholesaler, or retailer) and your role in that industry. Typical turns in inventories can range from 5 to 20 times a year, anywhere.

7. Number of Details in Receivables

By first calculating your average sales day, you determine the number of days in receivables-that is, the average length of time between selling a product or service and getting paid for it. Divide your total sales (from the P & L) by the number of days in that period (using 365 for a year). You divide that number into your current account receivables balance (from the balance sheet) after you have calculated the average day of sales. The resulting figure will give you the number of days of sales on your receivables.

Chapter 05: Tips for Managing Your Growing Business

For most small business owners, this transition isn't an easy one to make, and it involves adopting a number of new management skills that don't come naturally to many. This chapter offers a collection of time-tested tips that will help you work through this transition and manage your growing business better.

1. Focus on What You Do Best

How many small businesses do you know that are trying to offer too many services or products-more than they are able to deliver successfully? How many do you know that attempts to deliver the best quality together with the fastest delivery and the lowest prices-all at the same time? The successful small business is one that operates with the recognition that its resources are finite-that the business can only do so much, and still do so well. The business is therefore focused on what it does best; then, it is going forward and doing better than anyone else. Your personal resources are finite, and you can only do that much before you begin to do too much and lose focus. Keep your focus on what you can accomplish reasonably, leaving someone with something you can't do well. These tips to help you focus appropriately, and thus manage your time and talents better. An overflowing plate is a focal threat. You don't need all the people to be all things. Determine what you can delegate, to whom you can delegate it, and how quickly it will be required.

   a. When one project has to give way to another, make sure the first project is concluded temporarily at a convenient location. And follow a solid strategy for its resumption.

   b. There is a direct link between interest and focus. Don't expect to focus on themes that don't interest you for long periods of time. Delegate them to another body that is interested in such projects.

c. Focus, and the lack thereof, is a company culture-related issue. If you, the owner/boss, don't complete the projects you are starting or don't follow up on your initiatives, your employees will most likely behave the same way over time. Your lack of focus may result in their lack of focus; little will be done well or on time, and you'll be left with plenty of time to focus on your business' failure.

Best small business managers know dividends are paid for by the ability to focus. They've found that solving one problem is much better than having three problems in different stages of irresolution.

2. Bend the Rules when Necessary

A Small Business is a place Katharine Hepburn would have undoubtedly enjoyed. You may recall that Hepburn was once quoted as saying: "If you obey all the rules, you miss all the fun." We certainly aren't suggesting that rule-bending be considered lightly. Those for whom the rules are bent need to understand why the rules are being bent, and that the bending is an exception. The same holds true for when the rules need to be bent because of circumstances rather than individuals. When people and institutions become perfect, and problems become predictable, rigid, and inflexible rules may work. Until then, however, flexibility is the key to making the best of any imperfections.

3. Hold Your Employees Accountable

The best teacher you ever had? The chances are that the teacher made you accountable -accountable to do your homework, to participate in class, and to pay attention to whatever it was he or she happened to be teaching.

When the teacher told you to do something, by golly, you did it. In the process of making you accountable, this teacher no doubt communicated to you in advance what would happen if you didn't do what was asked of you.

Conversely, he or she also told what would happen if you accomplished what was requested. So, you knew exactly what to do and exactly what to expect in terms of reward or punishment. Most importantly, you knew that the teacher would follow up his or her words with actions. You could control the outcome by your choice to follow or not follow instructions. Somewhere along the line, your best teacher had discovered the necessary role of accountability in attaining desired results. Two elements make up this process of establishing accountability: a. Communication of expectations b. Follow-up Without the two workings in unison, you can forget about accountability.

And the lack of accountability will result in spotty performance at best, and at worst, no performance at all. Most small businesses can't afford continued poor performance. The same tools that worked for your best teacher can also work for you. If your employees aren't held accountable for their actions, they usually won't succeed. And, in the long term, if your employees don't succeed, your company won't, either. The time-tested "win-win" formula won't kick in unless both sides are involved.

4. Consider the 80-20 Rule

The 80-20 rule is alive and well in the small-business world. Consider the following examples of the 80-20 rule:

- **The 80-20 rule for your customers:** Eighty percent of your profits come from 20 percent of your customers. What this means to you: Focus your time and energy on those customers who have the potential to be profitable. Stop wasting your time on those who don't.

- **The 80-20 rule for your employees' output:** Eighty percent of your company's output will come from 20 percent of your employees. What this means to you: Work harder to improve, or cull, the 80 percent that isn't contributing and take good care of the 20 percent doing so much of the work.

- **The 80-20 rule for your employee problems:** Eighty percent of your employee problems come from 20 percent of your employees. What this means to you: Do something about that 20 percent. Either solve their problems (by training or motivating them) or solve your problem (by replacing them).

- **The 80-20 rule for your expenses:** Eighty percent of your waste comes from 20 percent of your expense categories. What this means to you: Focus on the 20 percent -that's where your leverage lies for increased profitability.

- **The 80-20 rule for your accounts receivable:** Eighty percent of your slow pay dollars come from 20 percent of your customers. What this means to you: Determine the source of that 20 percent; you usually find a common denominator. One salesperson, maybe? One product? One market?

- **The 80-20 rule for your success:** Eighty percent of your successes will come from 20 percent of your efforts. What this means to you: Find out how to leverage your talents as well as your time. Find a way to spend more time on the things you do well (and that benefit your business) while delegating those things that you don't.

5. Sleep On Important Decisions

Following is the guidelines to be observed by the president of the United States when there is a significant decision to take.

These Guidelines also apply to General Motors Chairman and Acme Plumbing Chairman. You should also apply these to your business decisions:

- Be steady. That is what Americans want most from their president, and what adversaries respect most.

- Do not get caught up in the event. History is full of presidents who were obsessed with a crisis or an impending decision, and made a bad choice as a result.

- Don't behave until you have to. The greatest dangers in a crisis are rash decisions based on emotion and insufficient information.

- Converse, think, and negotiate. Take your time, weigh all the possibilities, and don't jump into something you'll regret later.

The underlying strategy for all presidents of large and small organizations here is to stay cool, stay in control, and allow plenty of time to reach a decision. Wait until it subdues your emotions before making important decisions. Whether or not you like it, the biggest decisions in life and business usually only come about once. You're rarely allowed a second chance. "Tomorrow I'll be coming back to you" are the words for those times of making-it - or-break-it. Then head home. Take something tall and cool for a drink. Go and take the kids for a bike ride. And, on that, sleep.

6. Resolve Conflicts

The meek may inherit the earth, but at the same time, their employees may rebel. Employees are actively involved in the conflict. The more staff you have, the more conflict that you'll have to deal with. The stakes involved in that conflict are also becoming more important and the antagonists are becoming more professional at that conflict as the business grows. Good administrators also need to be competent problem solvers.

Conflict and its quick and easy to resolve do not come naturally to most people. Conflict resolution almost always calls for compromise and understanding in the heat of emotion, something many people cannot or will not do. The best way to resolve disputes? Let's face it. Immediacy. Conflict festering is always worse than conflicting again. Don't let yours become either cold or old.

7. Accept that Perception Is Reality

The message you send is important as a small business owner. Imagine the following scenario: Annual time has come for the performance review. On the far side of your desk, one of your employees fidgets nervously. You start the review with a complimentary remark and then dive into the presentation's guts. Your goal? For improving the performance of that employee. Your employee storms out of your office ten minutes later, slamming the door behind his. He thought you were personally attacking him.

And so works perception. Diddly-squat does not mean facts and intent. It's the only perception that counts-and that perception is reality until it changes perception. What, then, do you ask?

• When you lead people (as small business owners are supposed to do), it doesn't matter what you think or believe. What counts is what your workers consider you believe or think. If they perceive you are not giving a hoot about their problems, they're not going to give a hoot about their problems. If they feel that quality isn't important to you, then quality won't matter to them. If they perceive that you think the customer is a pain in the rear, the customer will be there for them.

- The presentation is key. Review to the employee? Meeting with shareholders? Presentation to the Customer? Talk about the association? What you intend to communicate here isn't the issue; what counts is the way your presentation is perceived.

Consider this: Ask a selection of your employees (allow anonymity, of course) how they view you and your business. Ask them for a 1-10 rating on anything you consider important to your company's success. Ask about cultural issues, management issues, leadership traits, ethics, individual respect, customer responsiveness, confidence, follow-up, accountability, focus-whatever perception you want to measure. Compare the scores of your staff to yours instead. Do their perceptions correspond to yours? Our assumption? It's not even close on some issues. Like it or not, facts don't matter at all when it comes to dealing with people or being dealt with by people. What counts is perception.

8. Follow Many Rules Reasons

If your business is successful, there are myriad reasons for that success. You've hired right and fired right, focused, made a great product, or provided a great service, set up, planned and strategized the right distribution system, managed your cash. The list of things you did right continues forever. And if your business is in trouble, you will find a number of reasons for this as well. You've hired poorly, and you haven't fired when you should, your product quality is poor, your sales force needs training, your culture lacks accountability, you have an inventory-filled warehouse that won't sell. You get that idea.

That's how the Many Reasons Rule works, and it applies to everything you do, whether it's running your business, raising your kids, or shuffling along life's backroads. So what does this? Do many Reasons rule mean when your company hits one of the many speed bumps on the road to success? It means there are no easy fixes.

Sure, you have priorities, but tomorrow your company won't do a flip-flop simply because you've put in place a quality program, started a program to improve your hiring techniques, decided to install accountability in your culture, or whatever you've started doing that you haven't done before. And it means the winner in the small-business game is the owner who has discovered it's all that makes the difference-the big things and the little things and all the things in between. Success is the fruit of all that you do.

Conclusion

A person has a passion or any motivation this for starting up a business. The next step is to create your business plan: here, you can map how your business will get to where you want it to be in three to five years. A business is less likely to succeed without a clear vision, yet it's surprising how many people start out without one. Contrary to the opinion many people have about the consultants; many also feel that a business plan is overwhelming and unnecessary. Or put it simply, a business plan is merely a compilation of your thoughts. You've already thought about why you believe your idea is going to be a success, and why people want to buy from you.

Starting a business will almost certainly require some form of financing, whether it is; a startup loan, a bank loan, an overdraft, or even a private investment. Finally, you need to ensure your finances are all in order before you start.

Cash flow is the number one reason, so many businesses fail so fast, and again, this is where planning comes in, which will be part of your business plan. This will mean updating an accounting and cash flow system, so you don't get lost in invoices and receipts and lose sight of your new business ' viability.

You need to understand the identity of your company at this point; the name and logo, for example. These need to stand out in the increasingly globalized and crowded market and be unique. It's a good idea to incorporate this image on a well-designed website before starting a business, and ideally, all of this needs to be completed before your business goes live. Hence the reasons why Entrepreneur does not run Small Business.:

- **Lack of Capital**

Of the vast number of small businesses that fail every year, nearly half of the entrepreneurs are responsible for lack of funding or working capital. In most cases, a business owner is intimately aware of how much money is needed to keep day-to-day operations running, including payroll funding, paying fixed and varied overhead expenses such as rent and utilities, and ensuring that outside vendors are paid in time. This disconnect leads to shortfalls in funding, which quickly put a small business out of business. Small businesses in the startup phase also face challenges when it comes to obtaining funding to market a new product, fund expansion, or pay for ongoing marketing costs.

- **Inadequate Management**

Another common reason small businesses fail is that a management team or business owner lacks business acumen. In some instances, the only senior-level personnel within a company is a business owner, especially when a business is in its first year or two of operation. Although a business owner may have the necessary skills to create and sell a viable product or service, he often lacks the attributes of a strong manager and the time required to manage other employees successfully.

Smart business owners outsource those activities that they do not perform well or have little time to carry out successfully.

A sound business strategy should include, at a minimum, a clear business description, current and future requirements for employees and management, opportunities and risks in the broader market, capital needs including expected cash flow and specific budgets; marketing initiatives; and competition analysis.

Business owners who fail to address the business needs within a well-designed strategy prior to commencing operations are setting their companies up for serious challenges. Similarly, a business that does not review an initial business plan on a regular basis, or one that is not prepared to adapt to market or industry changes, meets potentially insurmountable obstacles throughout its lifetime.

Until starting a firm, an entrepreneur should have a solid understanding of their market and competition to avoid risks associated with business plans. The specific business model and infrastructure of a company should be established long before products or services are offered to the consumer public, and potential revenue streams should be projected well in advance, realistically. The creation and maintenance of a business plan is key to the long term running of a successful business.

- **Marketing Mishaps**

Business owners often fail to prepare for a company's marketing needs in terms of capital requirements, prospect reach, and accurate projections of conversion ratios. When enterprises underestimate the total cost of early marketing campaigns, it is often difficult to secure funding or redirect capital from other business departments to compensate for the shortfall. Similarly, having realistic projections about target audience reach and sales conversion ratios is critical to the success of the marketing campaign. Businesses that do not understand those aspects of sound marketing strategies are more likely to fail than businesses that take the time to create and implement cost-effective, successful campaigns.

References

Thomasson, M. (n.d.). Managing Accounts Receivable and Accounts Payable in Modern Business. Retrieved from **https://invoicebus.com/blog/managing-accounts-receivable-and-accounts-payable-in-modern-business**

Gartenstein, D. (n.d.). How to Run a Successful Small Business. Retrieved from **https://smallbusiness.chron.com/run-successful-small-business-3183.html**

Rapetskaya, M. (3AD). 5 Things Not to Do When You're Running a Small Business. Retrieved from **https://www.entrepreneur.com/slideshow/306752**

Ward, S. (1AD). Reasons a Business Plan Is Key to Success. Retrieved from **https://www.thebalancesmb.com/why-write-a-business-plan-2948013**

ansson, A. (1n.d.). 7 Ways to Finance Your Small Business - bus. .com. Retrieved from **https://. business.com/articles/7-ways-to-finance-your-first-small- ess/**

How to Buy a Bus. · Everything You Need to Know. (n.d.). Retrieved from **http. w.fundera.com/blog/buying-an-existing-business**

Landau, C., Jarratt, L., Morgaine, iefels, J., & Angelique O'Rourke. (6AD). Palo Alto Soft. Retrieved from **https://articles.bplans.com/business-ideas, ps-to-starting-your-own-business/**

www.ingramcontent.com/pod-product-compliance
Lightning Source LLC
Chambersburg PA
CBHW070235220526
45465CB00004B/1430